New Money, New America

How to Scale Up in a Post-Pandemic World

by
Bryan Wood and Ryan Wood

Published by Finesse Literary Press
http://www.finesseliterarypress.com

Copyright 2021 Bryan Wood and Ryan Wood
The author of this Publication

All rights reserved. No part of this publication may be reproduced, stored in a retrieval system or transmitted in any form or by any means, electronic, mechanical, photocopy, recording or otherwise, without prior written consent of the copyright owner. Nor can it be circulated in any form of binding or cover other than that in which it is published and without similar condition including this condition being imposed on a subsequent purchaser.

The right of Finesse Literary Press' client is to be identified as the author of this work has been asserted in accordance with the Copyright Designs and Patents Act 1988.

A copy of this book is deposited with the British Library

Table of Contents

INTRODUCTION 5
IF YOU'RE HAVING A BABY, DO AN ULTRASOUND 9
RULE 1 17
BE PREPARED 19
THERE ARE NO SHORTCUTS 30
RULE 2 53
SHORTCUT TO HELL 56
THE WAKE-UP CALL 59
RULE 3 81
HOW TO PRINT YOUR OWN MONEY 87
1. A REASON WORTH PRINTING FOR 89
2. THE BETTER PLAN 94
3. SUCCESS GARAGE 99
4. IT'S THE FULFILMENT, NOT THE MONEY 103
MISTAKES ARE LESSONS, BUT DON'T MAKE
THEM TWICE 106
WHAT THEY DON'T TEACH YOU AT SCHOOL 110
WHY ENTREPRENEURS FAIL 119
MARKET FIRST 124
KNOW THE WATERS WELL 131
GATEKEEPERS EVERYWHERE 147
THE BIG LEAGUES WANT IN 150
BRYAN WOOD ON WHO IS AN
ENTREPRENEUR, REALLY? 154
WHO IS AN ENTREPRENEUR? 156
COVID AND ENTREPRENEURS 158

GEARING UP FOR A POST-PANDEMIC: BUSINESS IDEAS FOR THIS SEASON 161
THE DAWN OF A PANDEMIC 162
VIRTUAL BUSINESSES 164
DROP-SHIPPING 165
DROP SERVICING 173
FREELANCING 174
HIGH EARNING SKILLS 175
WEB DEVELOPMENT 176
COPYWRITING 179
TIPS ON BEING A GOOD COPYWRITER 180
PROS AND CONS OF FREELANCING 182
AFFILIATE MARKETING 185
HOW AFFILIATE MARKETING WORKS 187
AFFILIATE MARKETING CHANNELS 190
ADVANTAGES OF AFFILIATE MARKETING 192
DISADVANTAGES OF AFFILIATE MARKETING 194
VIRTUAL SERVICES 196
LOGISTICS 201
IT'S A WRAP 203

Introduction

We've wanted to write this book for ages. For a time too long, Bryan and I kept having that elusive dream of creating an autobiography, something we could leave to the annals of history. Sort of like our baton, our small yet timeless tome containing stories of our struggles and the numerous lessons we gathered along the way; rules and best practices gleaned from the comfort of our parents' home back in Maryland, to the streets where we sold candy and became president of the student council, to the life of an artist on the California road. In these pages, we share strategies that helped us and some situations that scared us. These anecdotes will undoubtedly help you make it big in whatever industry you find yourself, whether it's the music business, the world of art, or any other domain you can imagine.

For the most part, the project was delayed by our own procrastination. Finding reasons to not do it was a whole lot easier. We never said we wouldn't do it, instead always claiming that 'we'll do it tomorrow.' In our defense, we were quite busy, from performances to the intense demands of running several streams of business. All of these reasons helped us increase our skills in the realm of procrastination.

After a while, the idea of writing the book felt so distant, so daunting, that we just decided not to talk about it. It suddenly felt like we weren't cut out for it, like we were fish out of water, gasping for life in a foreign ecosystem. As rappers who punch down lyrics and create hit songs, you would think we would have it easy with cooking this book. They both involve the use of language, but that's all they share. We didn't have the writing skill, unlike the skill we developed while growing up: cranking out song lyrics. For artists like us, the last thing we wanted to do was punch down lines for a book. It wasn't something we enjoyed, not after spending hours crafting great lines for our music. In short, writing a book is not a joyous task, at least not for us.

However, we felt like we owed the world; we definitely owed our fans this, and so much more. We've always known we wanted to share our story with the rest of the world. We wanted our fans and kinspeople, especially African Americans, to find a way out of the rat race that ensnares most of the world's inhabitants. But even as rising stars, we still had our hiccups and roadblocks; we couldn't begin working on this book until late in 2019, when nobody saw COVID coming.

Bryan and I had one of those rare, emotional conversations about our deepest fears, and somehow, after that talk, we both decided it was high time we finally took up the pen, or the keyboard. And then, well, we stalled on it, again, through the dwindling remainder of the year.

Our procrastination was met by the bombshell; COVID struck, taking the planet by surprise. With the number of cases climbing high and business taking a sharp downturn, we were finally moved to take action. Apparently, this was the motivation we needed. One cold winter afternoon, Bryan and I sat down and looked that age-old thing called procrastination in the eye, and forced a deal with it.

"We're going to write this book, page by page," we told it, "and you're not going to interfere."

"What do I get in return?" it whispered in that otherworldly voice of absolute dread, creeping up our spines.

"We quit rapping."

We now present proof that we finished the book. And, well, we haven't kept our part of the bargain.

Sue us.

Before we continue, you should know that we do not claim to be experts. While we will cover several business topics and strategies, we'll be using our personal stories and beliefs to deliver the techniques and lessons that benefitted us throughout our journey. We'll share principles for the business world, and some intriguing concepts that can make your life more dynamic and productive.

You'll read stories our personal struggles at different stages in our lives, and we hope they inspire you to rise above what you think you can achieve. Most of what you'll find here will seem unlikely. Shocking, even. So, if you're looking for some candy-coated, five-easy-steps-to-make-millions garbage, you should probably toss this book in the dumpster and stick to your nine-to-five. This is no get-rich-quick scheme. If you're ever going to rise out of the trenches of poverty and mediocrity, understand this: there are costs to success. 'Something for nothing' is a façade. Ideas like the get-rich-quick plans will likely end with you deeper in the hole, and someone else pocketing your money as they leave. Real wealth has costs. Buckle up and settle in, because this is the ride of a lifetime, literally. We'll see you on the other side.

Cheers.

If You're Having a Baby, Do an Ultrasound

It was October 29th, 1977.

On a blisteringly bitter night just before the cold of winter arrived in earnest, the moon crept through the dark umbrella of clouds as Regina S. Wood screamed, agonizing over a sensation threatening to rip her insides apart. She was going into labor. After seven agonizing minutes, her husband, Willie B. Wood, finally managed to arrive outside the doors of a hospital in Tacoma Park, Maryland, his wife the suffering passenger. Regina was rushed to the ward while her husband remained distraught and frazzled, hurrying to park his dilapidated truck properly.

Inside the ward, Regina couldn't withstand the constant pain. Minutes bled into hours, but still no progress. The doctors had reached the unfortunate conclusion that the baby wouldn't come out. Not naturally, at least. They reached out to Mr. Wood, who was perched nervously outside the ward, practically shaking with fear and adrenaline. They informed him that an operation would be necessary to complete the delivery.

"Absolutely not," Mr. Wood declared stubbornly, his eyes going sharp, fingers folding inward to forge a fist. He would not relent. No one was going to put his wife through that.

"Willie!" his wife cried from the room. Each of her calls added to her husband's fear, until the doctor finally allowed him entrance. Willie Wood was petrified as he approached her bed, walking on legs that would barely hold him up. There was his wife, attended to by a handful of nurses, her face caked in sweat and anger.

"I want it out," she blurted between sharp breaths of pain, snot dripping down her nose, her eyes drooping on the edge of consciousness. "Get it out of me, Willie! I want it out now!"

She was too exhausted to hold any discussion. Her face was pale and sweaty under the mighty light strewn above the bed.

"You'll be fine, honey. You'll be fine." His words felt empty even as he tried to deliver them with confidence.

"I'm not." She shook her head, sweat drenching her dress and the bed underneath. "I'm not fine, Willie. Why...why is it taking so long?" Her teeth gritted between words.

"They're saying they..." Her husband exhaled, still trying to grapple with the sight and the implications. He had never seen such pain in all his life. Ever. His heart felt the pain beneath his sweat-drenched work uniform. "They're saying they'll have to cut you open. I can't allow that—"

"Willie…"

"Sweetie, I know you're in pain. You'll get through this."

"Willie," she said, writhing with an agony that restrained the movement of her lips, her words weakening, becoming whisper-like. Willie regretted getting her pregnant, putting her through this ordeal. Was this what it was like? Such agony. That women have been pulling it off for the entirety of human history; the realization of their strength was evident.

"Willie," she whispered.

"I'm right here, sweetie. Right here," Mr. Wood said, unable to find any other words.

She clutched him, her muscles jittery, and an inferno of pain brewing in her eyes. She opened her mouth once more, resolution etched into her face.

"Let them cut me open."

*

Mr. Wood had to be ushered out, his fists pounding against the ward's entrance as his wife's demands were communicated to the doctors. He face clearly displayed the panic and fear, and his eyes remained angry. He pounded the doors incessantly, pleading for the doctors to stop. They couldn't do this. They mustn't. They were really going to cut her open!

Exhausted, Mr. Wood paced around in a dazed stupor, his eyes swollen and irritated from sweat and tears. He had friends who needed a C-section, and it all had ended in disaster. They'd lost the child and the mother. Both gone in an instant. Those thoughts spiraled in his head, and he could barely stay sane as the hours grew long, no update coming from the delivery room. It was as quiet as a sealed morgue, he reflected.

And it disturbed Willie B. Wood to no end.

At 10:21 pm, a sharp wail filled the stale air; a loud, almost heavenly cry pierced Willie's ears. Astonished, he dashed towards the door, wide-eyed, his jaw hanging wide. His heart melted, and his eyes began to water anew. Was that…his baby? He watched a doctor wrap the child in a towel for cleaning. The doctor was looking out at Willie, child in hand. He could feel the tremors race up his spine as his head spun with joy. The doctor had two fingers raised. Peace, you can come in now, Mr. Wood thought, his grip shaky as he reached for the door.

"My god, Gina," he said to the mother who was still perched on the bed, nurses probing her insides. He was met with a frown from the doctor, who was no longer holding the child. The doctor had reached him, as did a nurse with golden, wavy hair, both of them shaking their heads and hands up.

"You can't be in here now," the doctor said through his medical mask while a nurse led him back to the door.

"But she's done. She's done. You said to come in—"

"Mr. Wood, please, you cannot be in here. We'll be done in a bit," the doctor said as the nurse kindly ejected him back into the cold hallway.

"I don't understand. You said to come in," Mr. Wood said, panic taking its hold once more. "Is something wrong with my Gina? Is she okay?"

Mr. Wood's vision seemed to swim as the memories of his friends returned. Medical staff were gathered, circling his wife, their movements quick, almost frantic, Willie thought. Something was up. Something.

As the doctor exited the room once more, Willie had him cornered. "What's happening to my wife?" Although it was a question, it sounded as if it demanded an answer that couldn't come fast enough.

"Did you do an ultrasound?" the doctor asked with the usual stoic resolve necessary for a successful career in medicine (or any service industry).

"What?"

"Mr. Wood, did you take your wife for an ultrasound to check on the progress of the pregnancy?"

Mr. Wood shook his head. In those days, an ultrasound was pretty expensive. It wasn't something a local warehouse truck driver could afford.

"There's been a change in plans," the doctor said, and Mr. Wood braced himself for what was to come…and failed. His knees shook and his hair stood on end, because nothing could have prepared him for it.

The doctor pulled down his mask, revealing a smile tugging at the corners of his mouth as he began to explain. However, before he could, a second piercing cry echoed from the room. Mr. Wood flinched toward the window, confused.

"Mr. Wood," the doctor said, pulling off his surgical gloves, "congratulations. They're boys."

Mr. Wood's face remained frozen, stuck in a perpetual state of shock. As those words reached the parts of his brain responsible for the interpretation of meaning, all time seemed to freeze. His face, and his heart, morphed through a thousand and one expressions and emotions, all of them seemingly numbed as the world continued to spin. He strode towards the window area, his eyes searching for the confirmation.

"T—twins?" he said, working the muscles of his mouth, tongue and vocal cords with some difficulty, his gaze resting on the seven-pound infant caked in goo, screaming his lungs out.

As Mr. Wood would later find out, one of the twins had been stuck in the womb with the umbilical cord wrapped around his neck, hence the C-section. The twins had emerged about one minute apart, with Bryan Keith Wood coming out first, followed by Ryan Kenneth Wood.

That night, Mr. Wood tried to sleep in his truck, but he was too shaken from the day's events to rest peacefully. In the end, he gave up on sleep and slouched, arms folded, in the back compartment of his truck, brooding. He had a couple of orders to deliver in a few short hours, but all of that would have to wait a while, it seemed. There was a new addition to the family, a new dynamic. And not just one. Two chocolate bundles of wonder. Two extra mouths to feed, to share their little home in rural Maryland. Two infants who would grow into power twins, rocking the music industry with their genius and entrepreneurial skills. But old Mr. Wood couldn't see that yet. Perhaps he did; we can't really tell. All we know is that he sat there, thinking, praying as he watched the stars, waiting for the sun to paint the sky with its soft, spreading light so he could see those wonder boys up close.

"Goodness. Twins," he muttered to himself and the wind. "What am I to do with them?"

RULE 1

Our birth story was a near disaster. For hospitals, doctors, and expecting parents that are ill-prepared for such scenarios, disaster can certainly strike. Not every hospital around the world has the resources required to maximize positive outcomes. Each one carries the noble cause of preserving human life, but often they can lack both manpower and infrastructure. In the not-so-buoyant states of Africa, chances for success can be slim.

Imagine the emotion of the delivery room, your spouse requiring a C-section but you can't afford one, or the hospital can't afford a practitioner skilled enough to perform it. This may seem far-fetched, we understand. Close your eyes, inhale, and think about it.

It is not a laughing matter to set aside.

The repercussions of such a scenario are downright scary. Losing a child and her mother; a moment more cruel may not exist. Yet, in some parts of the world, this is the reality. We could have had the same experience. Our dad could have lost his family. Think about the consequences of not having the proper equipment, the qualified practitioners, the bank account, and the emotional cost; what it would cost you as one full-grown, breathing, thinking bag of meat and consciousness.

Thoughts like these can be uncomfortable, but think of them as manure, a sort of fertilizer for insightful and rich thinking. Consequences to any situation can be great, and pondering them has helped the human species evolve into intelligent, self-correcting creatures, allowing them to right wrongs, to avoid previous mistakes, and to prepare for the many more that life throws your way. This only works if you take the time to think, consider, and empathize. And it is on this idea of thinking that we shall open the floor.

If there's one sure way to get ahead in life, whether it's starting a business, competing in a sport, preparing for an epidemic or, perhaps, you've been smacked by an epidemic and you're trying to get back on your feet, it's to follow our first rule:

BE PREPARED

That's it. There's no path to success if you're slurping around, waiting for a magical genie to grant you three wishes. That's fantasy stuff. And this—right here, before your face—is real life. There are no filters, no "aww-he's-just-a-first-timer-let's-take-it-easy-on-him" nonsense. The world outside of your home doesn't care about you, and wants to eat you up. It is anything but gentle. It is brutal and spontaneous, programmed to drive you to the extremities of madness and its several cousins. And the only way to win the game of life, as it is currently played, is highlighted in this sacred two-word sentence:

STAY PREPARED

As mentioned earlier, our species has had to consistently evolve. We did stuff. Terrible things, and then we made adjustments. This cycle has repeated non-stop since the beginning of human history, from clans to public institutions to private companies, you name it. There's always been a culture of preparation, and it's downright foolish to jump into something without taking preparation measures.

But how? How can one stay prepared in a world as malevolent, unpredictable and chaotic as ours? No one saw COVID coming. No one sensed the economic meltdown approaching. You might say, "I'm dead broke, I just lost my parents, I just got fired. How does anyone prepare for that?" Well, calm down, Mr. I-Didn't-See-It-Coming. Mr. Wood never saw it coming either. But he could have.

While he whined and groaned in the back seat of his truck, he was wasting precious time and precious sleep, something that would affect his productivity in the next few hours when it would matter, which would only lead to more mistakes.

Listen, whining is no way to steel yourself. Neither is avoiding responsibility for your lack of foresight into your situation. Don't be like our father in the late hours of October 29th, 1977, all cramped up in his truck and panicking over his new set of twins. Now, we still love our dad, despite his mistake. He means so much to us and we doubt we'd ever have made it this far up the status ladder if it hadn't been for his tremendous wisdom and tutelage over the years. Dad was a godsend when we needed to learn how to be street-smart. Growing up in urban areas, he had had to fend for himself since the age of eleven. He pulled himself through school and, having done a series of odd jobs along the way, finally built his own house with savings he had accrued. No handouts, no magical genie.

Dad was always our champ. As was Mum. However, the truth is that in the hours immediately after our birth, he was troubled. Scared. He was gripped by that deep, hidden tension that has always existed and thrived in the troubled souls of men. That dark feeling that has driven kings mad, pushed some towards death and others, insanity. It is called fear. And it was seizing control Mr. Willie B. Wood's head while he was curled up in his truck, leaving him unable to prepare for his new set of challenges.

How did this happen? How was it even possible? Two entire human beings. That nursery room at home now needed another crib. How would he feed them, guide them through two sets of education, two graduations? And then there was college tuition, and then…goodness, what had he done?

We suspect these were the thoughts zipping through Willie Wood's mind on a constant loop. Can we blame him for his mental weakness in this moment? No. He is mortal. And, like the rest of us, he is susceptible to the allures of human nature, to fear and despair. And these are simultaneously our greatest allies and greatest foes on the journey out of the depths of poverty.

Willie Wood did what anyone who had been plunged into this uncertain reality would do. He reacted, brooding about how he would feed the two extra mouths that had joined the Wood family. Where did this all go wrong? Well, we would say it's pretty simple; he didn't see two coming. He couldn't afford an ultrasound. And when it came to making a safe, smart family decision, doing an ultrasound was all that mattered.

What if he had ordered an ultrasound? What if he'd found the money and received the forewarning that his wife, our mother, was expecting twins? Would he have used the information to prepare? Would he have been well rested and supercharged for the job ahead of him?

Well, of course!

Because, the following day, Mr. Wood would earn a business deal that would change the entire course of his career. A new company would be acquiring the factory where he worked and he was likely on his way to a promotion, moving from an entry-level truck driver to managing the company's sea of drivers. Dad was street-smart, charismatic and knew how to get things done. Stuff like that caught the attention of his supervisors, and they were about to call Willie Wood up to their table when his wife was put to bed. With two seven-pound boys and debts piling up, his promotion was suddenly in jeopardy.

The weight of the situation strained the new father as he pondered his possible solutions. Yes, he was getting a promotion, but what if he failed? What if he got fired? There was suddenly an extra person that he would be letting down. Our dad is strong-willed and probably the most lethal-looking man there is on this planet, but on that day, on October 29th, 1977, he wasn't looking like the champ we would know him to be. He was losing the confidence battle after having lost the preparation fight. Losses come quickly when you're not prepared. You get punched in the mouth, and the world tumbles out of your line of sight.

Life can be quite unpredictable. You may assume events will unfold in a particular fashion and then *boom!* Your notion of an accurate prediction is gone and all of your metaphorical eggs are staring up at you, their yellow and oily fluids squashed out of their shells and splayed across the ground, like something from a horror movie. However, unpredictability doesn't change the fact that preparation is just as necessary to winning in life as oxygen is to the human body.

Being prepared is a concept far beyond accomplishing a task or two. There's a lot of psychology to it. Take basketball, for instance. You don't dribble aimlessly during a game just to show off unless you're Steph Curry or Jordan, which you're not. There's a mission you are trying to complete. Stop your opponent and put the ball in their basket. To this end, basketball coaches don't just roam the streets and pluck a couple of strangers off the sidewalk, throw them in oversized jerseys and order them to jump around the court. No. You have to be prepared.

Height. Stamina. Speed. Coordination. These are the ingredients of basketball talent. But even the ingredients aren't enough. How do you learn to cultivate these ingredients? Your cultivation happens at the preparation ground, where you're sweating, acquainting your limbs, mind, and body with the rules of the game. You're learning how to shoot, defend, and dribble, all of which impacts the singular objective of winning a game—not just for you, but as a team. You're learning how many babies to expect and how to handle them. Preparation is a beautifully poetic kind of ultrasound.

Dad shared the story of our birth with us when we reached the age of six. We were seated by his feet, Bryan and I, our eyes wide as our minds reeled with the movie playing in our imaginations. The movie of our birth as told by the man himself, Willie Wood. Dad said he didn't recover from the shock of having twins until the following evening. And, it had nearly cost him his job. Our father had been all nerves the whole time, contemplating how they were all going to pull through.

But what does preparation have to do with anything, you ask? It's everything.

Imagine you wanted to build a house. Do you just find a flat spot on the ground, start digging and arrange some bricks? Do you just keep pushing forward until you run out of money and resources? You could, but the result would most likely end in disaster. Preparation lets you know what you're getting into. It will inform you on what it will cost to raise the house and install the necessary structures. And yes, preparation does take effort.

Preparation is sweating on the practice court, perfecting a move, failing and failing until you're sure you can execute it with your eyes closed and twenty thousand people screaming at you. It is having an ultrasound way before your wife screams in the middle of the night over broken water.

Ever heard about how Isaac Newton came to discover the concept of gravity? He was sitting under an apple tree one day when, *boing!* An apple fell hard on his head and then, *aha!* He had it. The genie had struck him with a beautiful gift and said, "Hello there, please take this concept about gravity and populate scientific minds with it."

Of course, that isn't exactly what happened. Oversimplified by history, the narrative has been that Isaac Newton had been lucky, that the apple striking him was some divine orchestration engineered to hand deliver the concept of gravity into his hands. But this isn't the case, at all. Maybe there are lucky coincidences from time to time, but this isn't one of them.

The story was more accurately explained in a 2010 publication of the *Independent* written by Steve Conor. Mr. Conor explains that the simplified story only seemed to rub off as true due to man's unending joy for attaching spiritual or unusual explanations to events. He goes on to explain,

> "It was 1666, and the plague had closed the most of public buildings…Newton had to abandon Cambridge for Woolsthorpe Manor, near Grantham in Lincolnshire, the modest house where he was born to contemplate the stellar problems he had been pursuing at the university. He was particularly obsessed with the orbit of the Moon around the Earth and eventually reasoned that the influence of gravity must extend over vast distances. After seeing how apples always fall straight to the ground, he spent several years working on the mathematics showing that the force of gravity decreased as the inverse square of the distance."

The excerpt hammers on the point that Newton had been working on something related to the problem of gravity well before the apple moment occurred. Let's say a genie had really appeared to young Mr. Newton while he was walking to the university. The genie extends its hands, smacking Isaac's head with an apple. Newton would have had no inclination regarding the nature of gravity or how it relates to the mystery of objects being attracted by a centrifugal force towards the earth. If he had been like us and been smacked by that genie, he'd say, "Well, what did you do that for?" Then, like us, he would probably attempt to retaliate and smack the genie with the same apple.

But note that the article excerpt explains how long Newton had been working. He had been contemplating a problem and then observed the falling of apples. Newton had been studying the concept of gravity and kept wondering, *what is this? Why can't we just fly up, floating skywards every time we jump?* And then, that infamous morning arrived. It was just another day for Newton when the sun rose. They even had an epidemic taking place. A plague. And it was on that seemingly ordinary day that all his failures at attempting to understand the gravity phenomenon finally made sense. All the crumpled papers, the burned-out candles, the heavy eye bags and insomnia were all worth the trouble. Because a singular apple fell off a tree, bringing sense to all the seemingly fruitless preparations he had been conducting and then, *boing!* Hallelujah! Gravity is understood!

Too often, we can't comprehend the preparation behind an event taking place. We think that if only we was as fast as Usain Bolt, we could make a run for the bank and dash off with the money. They'd never know what hit 'em. Or, if only we had voices like India Arie or Beyonce, we'd be a little better off. Well, guess what? Nobody starts better off. No one is handed their talent. Everyone worked for what they have. Usain Bolt grew up racing with a cheetah. Yes, a cheetah. So, it doesn't matter where you are on the status ladder; you have to be prepared. Know your stuff. Find out what you're getting yourself into. Do your homework. Study those that have what you want and understand how they got it.

Like Newton, situations in life won't always make sense. You'll probably fail on numerous occasions. But don't worry. It's normal. Just pay your dues, in the form of preparation. Gear up and lean into the clumsiness and blindness of it. You may be shocked, perhaps overwhelmed, by what lies in store. Maybe you'll be expecting twins. Maybe you'll find that you have a handicap and you have to make up for it with ten times the gritty effort. Maybe you can channel that handicap into a superpower that others cannot fathom. Perhaps. But whatever you do, don't be like Willie Wood, who didn't do an ultrasound. Mr. Wood, who had a chance to see the problem moment coming and passed. Your ultrasound may be sitting down to write out your dreams, or plot out a strategy to solve a problem. We don't know how bad it is and the truth is that we don't care. Okay, we do care, but our caring isn't going to solve your problem. Get up and work. Prepare.

Prepare.

There Are No Shortcuts

It had been just another autumn day, the sky crystal clear as a cool breeze rushed through a small window of our parents' apartment in Maryland. We were twelve, an age when a lot had been going on at school and somehow, at the beginning of our struggles with the world around us, we felt out of key. Like the world was singing its song at a pitch we couldn't hit. Our outfits, how we walked, everything about us didn't ring of class or respect. As our peers would come to say: "we didn't got no swag." On this otherwise ordinary day, we had come home from school with the beginnings of a plan. Mum happened to be home earlier than usual, and Dad wouldn't be home until later in the evening.

"You go tell her," I told Bryan, who gave me a sharp look of refusal.

"You can either tell her or we forget about it."

"Don't chicken out," I said. Maybe more shaming would move him to action.

"You're the chicken."

"Come on, Bry," I said. "This is our only shot at explaining why we need it."

"I'm not talking." Bryan folded his arms, still lying on the rickety wooden bunk bed in those oversized pants he'd just worn to school. I had the same pair, and mine weren't looking exactly presentable either.

"And here I thought you were the brave one."

"Haha, nice try, Ryan. Not working."

"Okay, okay," I said, sinking into the lower bunk. "You are such a loser."

"Good thing I'm a twin. I am not alone."

"Shut up."

"Or?"

"I'll hit you…in the face."

"Yeah, come on, give it a try," he said, sliding to the edge of his bed, his face visible just above me. One of Bryan's many talents was how he could made you feel stupid for some of your worst ideas. It was that devilishly annoying grin.

"You know I can, right?"

"Good thing we both have hands," he said, bringing his knuckles down to my nose.

"Man, your hands smell like a dumpster," I joked, watching him reach behind him for something. Before I could blink, he smacked his pillow against my face, letting out a silly laugh of triumph. I attacked with my pillow in retort; the two of us temporarily forgot about our cares, messing around until we could hear Mum screaming that we'd better keep our voices down.

Mum was glaring hard at us over the thick leather book in her hands, her glasses poised on the bridge of her nose at an angle, signaling that they were close to falling off.

"You boys are kidding, right?" she said with a look that was anything but jovial.

I swallowed and tried to respond, but Bryan was faster.

"We're not. The kids at school have a lot of cool stuff. But us," he said, looking at me, "we look—"

"Renegade," I blurted.

"Old school," he said, shooting a scowl my way. "With that kind of money, we could get some pretty cool stuff, and then, maybe, everyone might like us."

Mum let out a laugh as she set the book aside. I'll never forget the look on Bryan's face as we watched her laugh like we had said we'd swallowed the moon.

"You boys, you'll be the end of me," she said, somehow lovingly. "Come here, come…Bryan, Ryan…"

We strode toward her with mixed feelings. She made us sit on either side of the couch, her hands resting on our heads.

"I see you boys are really starting to grow. You want to belong."

"We want to be cool, Mum," I said.

"Is that what you call it now, being cool?" she said, beaming her toothy smile while Bryan rolled his eyes. "Five hundred dollars is a lot of money, boys."

"Yes Mum, but it'll really go a long way if—"

"There's no way your dad and I would hand over five hundred bucks for some feel-good trivia. Money doesn't grow on trees, boys."

"But, but, the kids at school. They keep laughing at us," I said, feeling my eyes moisten at her rejection.

"It's normal to feel as though you're not fitting in. Everyone struggles with being accepted, no matter how much money they have. I had my share growing up."

"That's not true, Mum." I shook my head, finding it hard to reconcile with the notion that our self-assured mum was ever a child who had experienced the social ex-communication that takes place when you don't fit the image everyone else expects you to.

"Oh yes, boys. I did," she said, squeezing our hands as she recounted a few stories to us. I kept shaking my head, though. It simply was not possible. Mother was only making up these stories to make us feel better, to convince us that we would be okay. She wasn't going to hand us the $500 we had asked for. She wasn't going to hand us any money. My cheeks felt hot at the thought, my eyes damp as an imaginary knot tightened in my throat.

"Mum, please," I said. "This means a lot."

"I know, sweetie. I know it does. Jeez, Ryan, are you really crying?"

"No," I said, sniffing back mucus as I wiped my eyes dry, but the tears only doubled back. "Yes, Mum, I'm—I'm crying."

Mother laughed and then rose from the couch, excusing herself for a moment. Bryan and I watched her walk off, her feet rhythmically pounding the stairs as she ascended. We heard the sound of her bedroom door close, which seemed to give Bryan an opportunity to talk.

"Nice drama. You made her change her mind already. Way to go." He looked excited as he congratulated me.

"I wasn't drama," I sniffed back, aching somewhere deep in my chest.

"Well, whatever it was, it worked. I bet she's gone to her room to bring us some cash. We're going to get those shoes!"

Watching Bryan get all giddied up made me smile. It was a sloppy, reluctant smile, but it felt good. I guess one of the rare features of being a twin is how you mirror the other's emotions, no matter how you're truly feeling. Seeing someone else with your face has a way of infecting you with whatever is coursing through their blood. Hopefully, it would be nothing venereal. Just kidding.

We sat up in the living room as we watched Mum return, a small jewelry box resting safely in her hands. Goodness, I thought, she was really going to give us the money after all. Returning to the couch where we waited, she set the box on the table, her gaze shifting back and forth from mine to Bryan's.

"You boys know what this is, right?" she said simply, betraying no emotion.

Bryan and I nodded. It was her jewelry box. She stored all her fancy necklaces and beads in there. Occasionally, she kept some change there, too. She considered it good luck to have a bit of money saved up in the house. I secretly thought she did this because the banks were all out to get your money.

"Know what's inside?" she asked, a small grin beginning to spread across her face. I nodded, surprised that Bryan didn't.

"What, Ryan? Tell it."

"Your grandma's necklace," I said.

Mother had a necklace she'd inherited from her mother, who had inherited it from her grandmother. It was an heirloom handed down to the women in her family. At its center, the necklace held a milky green pearl with small lines that bled into gold. Strewn across the length of the chain were round gemstones, seven of them in total. We had counted them a few times, Bryan and I, almost like a rosary. Whenever Mum wasn't home, we would sneak up to her room, prop open the box and sort through some of the spare change and bits of jewelry we knew to be in there. It was always tempting to make a run with those things, but we couldn't. Mother trusted us. She had even let us know where she kept the box; her trust was that strong. We could never make a run with anything of hers, though. The guilt would have killed me.

Mum nodded to confirm that my response was correct. She knelt behind the small table, then turned the box so that it faced us.

"Are you ready?" she said, her hands propped on both sides of the box like a game show host. I leaned forward, ecstatic that she would give in to our pleas and give us $500 for some cool designer clothes and shoes. My mind raced with the things our classmates would say when they saw us.

The box clicked open and in that instance, I froze. My eyes went wide, confusion bringing my brain function to a halt. What in the world was I seeing? Was this…real? Mum's face was plain as paper, like a sinister creature was looking back at us through those unblinking eyes. I glanced at Bryan, who didn't look as stunned as I was.

"Is that…for real?" I stammered, looking to Bryan, who remained silent.

The box was empty.

*

"Mum, I didn't do it."

Those words flew out of my mouth like missiles. I barely registered saying it, but I did, faster than I could stop and think. Mum watched me, a small smirk revealing itself at the corners of her mouth. It was then that I knew something was afoot. Bryan remained silent, seemingly unmoved by the events dramatically unfolding in front of us.

"Ryan," Mum said, walking around the small table and back to the side of the couch where I was seated.

"I didn't do it, Mum, I didn't do it," I said again, shaking my head as tears started forming in my eyes once more.

"I know you didn't," she said, her gaze panning towards Bryan. I followed her eye line, my lower jaw nearly detaching from my skull. Bryan stared back, still somehow unflinching. He knew something. Goodness, he knew something!

"Bryan?" Mother called.

"What?" he said, his mouth in a tight frown and his brows furrowing close together.

"You were in my room recently, weren't you?"

"Huh?" he said in that elusive, what-do-you-mean kind of way.

I sat there and watched the confrontation, stupefied. Could Bryan have been responsible? I shut my eyes, forcing the possibility from of my mind. How could I think such a thing about my twin? But again, the reality of it all was there, staring back at me, even with my eyes closed.

Mother had raised us to be gentle kids. We had a roof over our heads, clothes on our backs—though they weren't the fanciest clothes, they did the job—and we never went to bed hungry. Stealing wasn't a temptation we had to consider, since we had the few luxuries we could afford. And we were just fine with it, except that now we wanted to fit in with others who had more than we did. I watched mother stroll over to my brother, her hands resting on her hips as she waited for an explanation. He wore that rebellious look very well.

"Bryan," I whispered.

"*I* sold it."

Those words echoed off the walls, followed by the loudest silence I had ever heard. Oxygen found its way back into my lungs as the mounting tension had, at last, exploded, spilling relief through my veins like a cold shower. Now that I could breathe again, my eyes were on my brother, wondering whether I had heard correctly. It was entirely unexpected, but the three words had still been said. They were swimming down my eardrums, traveling to the region of my brain that translated sounds to meaningful concepts, where there currently seemed to be some sort of traffic jam. And the fact that those words had left my mother's lips made it even more stunning.

"I sold them," she said, "for you two."

Some weeks back, before school started, we noticed Dad was working long hours and Mum was antsy. Financially, we weren't doing well. The factory where Dad worked was a little behind on payment and the bills were accumulating. There was also the cost of our tuition that would soon come due.

One afternoon, Mum was preparing to go somewhere, but her destination was unclear. We hadn't returned to school because of those tuition fees and a few other things, so we were home the most time, studying or beating each other up, something that would feed our future interest for a life in the ring.

"Mum, where are you going?" Bryan asked while I was perched over some dense textbook I wanted to badly fling away but couldn't, because I might ruin it. I didn't have a lot of textbooks for home studies.

"Just have to do a few things, you boys stay home…and behave," Mother called as she shut the door.

"She left with that jewelry box," Bryan said after the door closed and we could no longer hear her footfalls outside.

"Nah."

"She did. I could see it popping up out of her purse."

"Whatever, Bry. Come help with these math questions, would you?" I said, as Bryan was pretty good with numbers. Math was quite his thing. For me, though, it was hell. Languages were more of my strength. We went over a few textbook questions, but Bryan kept bringing up the jewelry box. Eventually, we made our way into Mum's room, and sure enough, we couldn't find it.

"Told you," Bryan said.

"Well, Mr. Keith," I said, rolling my eyes as I mimicked a courtroom judge. I called him by his second name like I usually did whenever I had something sarcastic to say. "You might as well just call yourself a psychic—"

"We should get out, she's home," Bryan said, glancing out the upstairs window. We dashed out in time to avoid being spotted, although Mum seemed preoccupied, a little upset, as she entered. Dinner was quiet and when Dad returned, there wasn't much to talk about. Before the end of the night, we went into Mum's room while Dad was in the shower to ask her what was up. When we entered, we saw the jewelry box returned on the desk by her bed. It was open, with all of her precious jewelry in it. Eventually, we gave up checking on her, never checking the jewelry box again after that. The only change in our lives was that we resumed school the following week.

"But, you had it with you," I said, having narrated what I remembered of the box to Mum and Bryan. The empty box still rested on the table.

"I sold it two days later, sweetheart," Mother said.

She explained that she found a buyer, but the buyer priced it poorly. She gave up on selling it altogether, which explained why she had been upset when she returned. We had thought it was some argument she had with Dad, something we knew to be rare. But it turned out to be no argument. Some random individual had really tried to rip her off, to take a family heirloom away for mere pennies.

"So how did you manage to sell it?" I asked, my ears aching out of curiosity and guilt.

"The buyer came back. Paid double the price after I told him I was no longer selling."

We audibly gasped when she told us how much she received for it.

"But why, Mum? Why did you have to sell it?"

"You boys need to stop asking me questions like you're my fathers," she laughed as she sank into a sofa chair across the room.

"Come on, Mum, we want to know."

"Well, for one, we paid some debts off," she said, sighing, "but your school. Had to sell it for your school tuition."

I heard Bryan sniff. I looked his way and saw his cheeks drenched in wet, silver trails. I didn't know when the silver tracks appeared on mine, but we soon matched. All I can clearly recall was hugging her tightly.

"Thank you so much, Mum," I said, my face buried in her shoulder.

Knowing that she sacrificed the jewelry keepsakes from her mother so we could make it through school was both heart-warming and heart-breaking. Bryan and I knew just how much Mum cherished that gem.

"So you see, boys," she said, "I would really like to give you some money…but I haven't any. And I doubt your dad does either, unfortunately."

While I tried to pull myself together, Bryan leaned over to me. I looked over and he was there, gesturing for me to lean in close to him. I did, and he brought his lips to my ears, whispering so Mum could not hear. I nodded when he was done and turned to her.

"It's alright, Mum," I said. "You don't have to give us any money."

"We'll try and look for some work so we can make some of our own," Bryan blurted.

"Now, isn't that something?" Mum said, dabbing her eyes, a big smile spreading across her face.

That was how we started our first business. But, what did we do? Well, what else gets groups of kids bouncing with excitement? We'll tell you. It's not comic books. And it's not video games.

It's candy.

We sold candy to the kids in our neighborhood. It might sound fun, but in practice, it was not. In fact, the day we decided to begin our endeavor, Bryan laid in bed, dreading the prospect of the whole thing. Only an hour earlier, he and I had gone to the store to purchase the packs of candy, both of us jesting about how silly it was and who would outsell who. But now, here he was, the brain behind the whole operation, catching cold feet.

"If you don't get up, I'll have to eat all of this myself," I said, dangling the pack of candy in his face. He didn't buy my bluff, though. He was bored out of his mind, dreading the notion of selling a few dozen sticks of hardened, colorful sugar in exchange for a few pennies.

"Go on without me, Ryan," he said, curled up on the couch, his face buried in a cushion.

"Is something wrong?" I asked, feeling for his neck. His temperature was normal. "Bryan?"

"I'm fine, I'm just a little jittery," he sighed, "about the whole thing."

I smiled. "Actually, I am too."

"Really?" he said, looking up. His eyes were stained with trepidation.

"Bryan," I chuckled, "we're just going out to sell candy, not rob a bank."

"I know. It's just, have you thought about what the other kids will say?" Perception was still the problem. The other kids probably didn't have to work hard for their money.

"Who cares what they say? We're going to be making money, Bry! Real money! Isn't that exciting enough?"

A small smile curled up his chocolate face. I ripped open the plastic bag of candy sticks in a flourish.

"Look, here's cash, and more cash, and more cash," I said, stacking the candies, one by one, each of them representing a fraction of the money we were going to make.

"There you go, touch them," I said, piling them into Bryan's palms. "You feel them?"

He shrugged. "I guess so."

"In a few minutes, you'll be exchanging these for money, and in return, you'll be putting a smile on all those kids' faces. I doubt they'll even think twice about us selling stuff. They'll be jealous when they see us doing this. Trust me, Bry."

"I don't know if I want to do this, man—"

Blop!

I slipped one of the candies into his mouth.

"Now shut up and get out," I said, smiling, knowing it made him feel better.

"Alright." Bry was nodding as he stood up from the couch, smiling, one cheek swollen with candy. "Let's go sell."

And sell we did.

We went from street to street, knocking on every door, ringing every doorbell we could find. If you lived in our area of Maryland at the time, you would have spotted a pair of twin faces systematically making their way down your street, one home at a time, both of them flashing their best smiles while they asked whether you cared for some candy.

"It's just for a few pennies," one of us said.

"We're trying to raise some money, to help around the house," said the other.

"This would go a long way for us."

"Please, please, please."

We would blink those puppy eyes, our smiles spreading as far as we could stretch them. And it almost always worked. For the first few weeks, we were moderately successful. We were there making our bread. We were happy. However, there was a problem brewing. Business began to slow, as the folks in our neighborhood were getting tired and we were gradually losing our enthusiasm. The excitement from a new venture began to wane. We had to cook up a new strategy. After a day of brainstorming, we tried something fresh. We still went door to door to sell candy, but we decided expand our offerings.

"Hello Mrs. Grey," I would start. "Would you care for some candy?"

"It's okay if you aren't buying today," Bryan would go on. "We did notice your lawn could use a hand."

"We can help you take of it."

"At a really, really good price."

"What do you say, Mrs. Grey?"

Hearing those words roll from the lips of twin boys had a way of eliciting positive responses from folks and families we visited. Bryan and I would alternate lines from the script, each of us displaying our earnest faces while we made our pitch. And we almost always landed the sale. Before we knew it, we had swapped our candy sales business for managing the lawn care of people's properties. When we arrived home after school, or during the holidays, we went straight to the homes we managed, making sure they were in pristine condition. The great part about this line of work is that it almost advertises itself. Others can see the results and decide if they want to take part.

Soon, we were doing a whole lot more than just mowing lawns. We were raking leaves and shoveling snow, all within the little city of Oxon Hill, Maryland. We had about six houses on our list, and we were paid every week to maintain the landscaping, earning about $60 per house. It was the easiest money we ever made and at such a young age, it seemed like a significant sum.

The whole idea about trying to look cool and feel accepted seemed to have spurred us to take significant action. The progress felt rewarding. We felt valuable, efficient. Bryan and I kept up with school, as well. We studied harder and as soon as the bell chimed, we bolted, still energetic and motivated, straight home for a quick meal so we could hurry to our 'enlisted estates.'

We maintained those homes every season throughout high school, and their owners were enthralled with our work. They were happy to let us manage them for a very long time. When autumn arrived, we raked the leaves. During the winter months, when snow glazed the yards, we shoveled and scraped them. In summer, the grass grew quickly, so we would cut them regularly to keep them looking fresh.

Soon though, we determined we could be making more money, so we set out to do just that. As we started taking up those jobs, we didn't have to bother Mum or Dad about funds. Bryan and I even started saving, even if it wasn't as fun. We would split our earnings and save them separately. We wanted to see who could save up more while resisting the urge to buy things we didn't need. The competition was intense. It became so extreme that we actually had a few things we needed to buy, but neither of us would back down on the savings battle. Eventually, though, Mum just went through both our savings, retrieved the money we should have spent, and bought what we needed. We were angry initially, but she didn't care, and eventually we learned.

"You need to learn to take care of yourselves," she said. "Money doesn't have a value if it only sits there, doing nothing."

Those words struck a chord.

Bryan and I had to consider the wisdom of it and get to the bottom of the lesson. We had heard a few seminars about making your money work for you, but we never quite understood how to put the concept into practice. And the truth was that we wanted to make more money in as little time as possible. Bryan and I had thought about things people would pay lots of money for, things that others considered high in value. It didn't help that cleaning up people's property was starting to get boring. We wanted something that would allow us to move around a lot. Something that sold fast. And we found one such product.

Marijuana.

We knew it was wrong to sell contraband, especially the criminal risks we had to take, but being young boys with blood and curiosity pumping through our veins,

Bryan and I managed to get our hands on a few loads. We weren't exactly sure how we would pull it off, even after we acquired it, but to our surprise, we sold it fast. We went back for more and sold the next batch even faster. Predictably, though, we began to run into trouble. Before we could get situated, some of the junkies in the area began asking for some, and we weren't comfortable with them knowing about us. Word got out fast, which will happen when you do a good job, and we were starting to get sucked into the world of drugs. We would've been drug dealers. But, thankfully, another event knocked us off course.

Around that time, our school had arranged a field trip to the city's jailhouse. You know, just a little something to acquaint students with what life behind bars looked like. We were shaken to the core. We were taken to different jail cells and shown how prisoners slept. Goodness, we were even shown what they ate. Things got a little tense, at least in my head, when the doors slammed shut and we were locked in. The chills that rippled up my spine, I'll never forget. I probably peed my pants that day, as would any other kid. It was even worse for me knowing that I was doing something that could put me here.

It turned out that the whole event regarding the shutting doors had been planned, and soon everyone was laughing. Well, I wasn't laughing, and neither was Bryan. We thought something deeper was going on, that the authorities had somehow found out about how we sold marijuana. Goodness, they were going to lock us up, no matter how many times they joked about it! Those thoughts echoed in our heads, and I could see Bryan's eyes flicker with horror in that cell.

They did let us out, thankfully. And although they had held a warning-laden lecture in there, not a word of it managed to stick in our minds. Not because we were ignoring them, but because we no longer needed to be told what not to do. The experience was enough on its own. We decided that we'd had our first and last attempt at selling marijuana. Even to date, we can still recall what those cells looked like, and how we felt on the wrong side of those doors. They were cold, and the prisoners slept on concrete floors. They ate cheese sandwiches and drank water. It was a pretty provocative experience for two young minority boys, so we made sure that jail life stayed off the list of our experiences.

Rule 2

As humans, it's only natural to desire the fastest path to complete a task. We're wired to look for the easy way out. Lock two suspected thieves in separate cells and tell them each that they have three choices: either provide information on the other, confess to get a slightly shorter sentence, or spend a long time in an orange uniform. Any warm-blooded individual would rattle their mouth. Why? Nothing overrides self-imposed ideals and moralistic codes like the need for self-preservation. When faced with the toughest odds, we will always succumb to baser options. It's nothing personal or something to be ashamed of. It's human biology. And that's totally fine, except that it's not actually an eco-socially beneficial trait. It's stupid, childish, and a perfect way to live a pretty mediocre life.

The example of the suspects is a famous concept in psychology known as game theory. It's simply an experiment that tampers with a human's desire for self-immortality, but we digress. Everyone wants to make money. That's a given. And everyone wants it fast, no doubt. We want fancy clothes, classy outfits. We want to show off our cool rides, and do whatever we want. We may want it to help solve other problems. The quest for that quick surge of dopamine is addictive by nature, hence our desire.

Subconsciously, we keep looking for ways to do more. Get more. Be more. Some call it growth. Others, greed. As for us, we won't be a part of that syntax war, saying this one's good and that one bad. Instead, we'll approach the subject from a neutral point of view and let you decide where your line is.

Of course, having luxury items isn't bad, as long as it makes you happy, right? But again, having too much of a good thing can pose a problem, in that it can warp your perception of reality; numbing your ability to experience pain, thereby leaving you disconnected from one of the core aspects of humanity. The root of all addiction is a pursuit of some sort of high, something to help us feel better about ourselves, about the human condition. Emotional pain and lack of self-acceptance have been some of the leading causes of the supposed drive to success, to wealth. For Bryan and myself, we couldn't handle that we weren't, in the sense of the word, 'cool.'

Though we may not have known it at the time, as we doubt many do, it was fortuitous that we felt that way. It ultimately steered us towards taking responsibility for our finances. However, the downside became eminent when we garnered too much attention. We wanted to earn more so we could be cooler. We wanted quick cash so we wouldn't have to spend long hours cutting lawns and shoveling white ice that clung to the cold concrete.

We wanted our fix of good dopamine. And marijuana was our shot, we thought.

Of course, we were tempted to smoke our product on more than one occasion. But we knew it wasn't for us. Besides the fear of having to look Mum and Dad in the eye and have them become aware of that faint smell of marijuana, we understood that the consequences would be severe, and we would be paying that price for a long time, if not permanently.

Shortcut to Hell

Most young folks out there are in a hurry. They want to make memories, make money, and travel the world. Don't we all want that? It is an idea circulated by Hollywood and the music industry (yes, we're probably guilty of this too), the idea that success is all about money and you better get rich quick or die trying. Pop culture, some may call it.

With ideas like this widely propagated by all facets of media, it's only normal that an individual's day-to-day grind becomes aimed at trying to get as much cash as possible in as short a period as possible, to reach that status they see others achieving. And this drive can pressure them to make terrible decisions. You've heard of people taking bizarre actions for that pay day. Human trafficking, drugs, prostitution, etc. If you're going to make it off the shores of poverty with a business model that will outlive you, you cannot be taking quick fixes, like marijuana, especially during or after a pandemic that is currently enveloping the whole world. For individuals hoping to make a mark, you have to look for problems worth solving. The emphasis is on the word 'worth.' Hawking marijuana, therefore, is no profession worth your time. Yes, you're helping people get high and escape the harsh claws of reality for a moment, but you're killing them, putting more junkies on the street, breaking up more families along the way.

The world will always need less of these kinds of people. There are homes devastated from the impact of COVID-19. People have died, millions have lost jobs, and a vaccine isn't going to bring it all back to normal. Instead of looking for some get-rich-quick scheme, what if you invested some time and brainstormed solutions to a problem that's been ravaging the world? What if you invented the new airplane that ran on less fossil fuel? What if you cooked up a solution that solves the problems we have with agriculture, doubling up the world's food production, thereby putting food on the tables of billions? Imagine how many people could turn away from drugs because they don't have any big stresses to run from. That could be your name in the history books.

Bryan and I had attempted the shortcut and I must say, we were awfully lucky to have had that change of mind before it was too late. That experience at the jailhouse changed the course our lives. We actually had the privilege of visiting a courthouse later that same day. Although Bryan seemed pretty certain that we weren't in trouble, that it was just a school trip, I still didn't trust it. My pulse was racing nonstop, and my classmates began to ask why I seemed so quiet. And sweaty.

"He's not feeling too well," Bryan said to cover for me, but he knew what I was thinking. He had the same terrifying thought, but he seemed to be handling it better. At the courthouse, we were allowed to sit in the back row for a few short hearings, watching people seated in the rows of chairs and benches, their faces a colorful rainbow of disgust, joy, horror and delight. We watched a few young men be sentenced. I will never forget a young and handsome twenty-one-year-old kid I saw. Goodness, the memory of it still haunts me. He'd been charged with murder, and I watched him be sentenced to life. I remembered thinking, "How could they let a kid so good looking rot away in a jail cell for the rest of his life? Just how?" The idea was nonsensical to me. It was so haunting that I started developing shock symptoms right on the spot, my skin cold and clammy, nerves shaking. Bryan took me aside, his hand on my shoulder.

"You're making a scene, Ry," he said, his gaze etched with concern. "You should use the bathroom."

I nodded, watching Bryan stroll up to the teacher leading us. Bryan told her I needed to use the bathroom and when I was finally in there, I filled my palms with tap water, washing my face. I looked around to make sure there was no one watching.

I wept.

The Wake-up Call

Taking a step back in time, our first real wake-up call came in 6th grade. We wanted to try out some new social situations that, for us, were foreign and uncomfortable. Specifically, Bryan wanted to dabble in school politics. There was a slot for the office of student council president back at Valley View Elementary. I recall thinking he was out of his mind when he first acknowledged his desire for the position. Knowing Bryan, I tried to give him time to think it through, believing he would get over the feeling in a few days. I thought it was some sort of fantasy, that he would come back to his senses and find that school politics wasn't the kind of life he truly wanted. Ultimately, I was the one who apparently needed to 'wake up.'

For days, Bryan talked about his plans to exercise that power of office, sometimes even making jokes about sanctioning me and some kids, when he became the president. I recall the surprise I felt on the day he raised his hand during the call for candidates. Seeing my brother dead serious about it, I wasn't sure I was excited for him or his prospects. I remember watching him sign up with dread in my heart, thinking, "How are you going to shuffle this with school work and everything happening at home?" I probably laughed when we left school that day, and maybe teased him a little on the way home. I quickly realized, though, he really was taking time to plan how he would win the kids' votes. I have to admit that I was skeptical. His plans would never work on the brats at Valley View Elementary. Having teased him a bit further about how hopeless he was, I agreed to help out. Did I have a choice?

We were sort of popular in school at the time. However, over time, all that celebrity had waned. Bryan and I had, in the preceding months, focused on school work and the after school gigs we had, so we weren't actively involved in the whole hey-look-I'm-cool contest that always took place even if you weren't participating. Being back to square one, Bryan and I knew we would have to take some serious action regarding our social standing if we were going to win the election. I say "we" because it felt like my fate was tied to his. With that in mind, we had some serious work to do.

The truth was that politics had never interested either of us before this moment, so we started out quite lost. We hardly spent time watching the news, or watching any election season. I recall asking Bryan every now and then, "What were you thinking?"

He would respond, "I have no clue," leaving both of us half giggling, half concerned over how we had gotten ourselves into this brilliant, terrible mess in the first place. Of course, it was all his fault, but we weren't trading blame at this stage. Being our first attempt at ever making decisions that would have an impact on individuals beyond our immediate circle, we knew we'd have to step up to meet the challenge.

Back at home, Bryan and I considered handing out flyers similar to the strategies of other students, but we remembered how we felt whenever we received those pieces of paper. It wasn't an experience we enjoyed or felt excited about, but we also had no other ideas. Seeing we didn't have much going for us, we were near giving up. On that fateful day, having returned home after a long, unproductive school session and a few appointments at the homes we managed, we sat in silence. Mum was out of town for the evening so Bryan and I, our heads running all sorts of equations that could translate to some real support, were coming up empty.

We heard Dad's truck pull into the driveway, but remained seated when the door opened, his long and sturdy frame strolling in, the door clicking shut behind him as his long, powerful and balanced strides shortened the distance between him and the other rooms.

"Hi, Dad," we called, flashing him half-hearted smiles. We waved and he nodded as he always did whenever he was too tired to converse. Minutes later, we heard the shower running in the bathroom, so Bryan went to the fridge to retrieve and prepare Dad's dinner. While his food was heating up, it would still be a while before Dad came to eat. Strangely, he received a phone call as he was finishing up with the shower.

"Hey Kenneth, Keith," he called to us after hanging up the line. "Get down here. Your mum wants to talk."

Dad was still in his towel when we reached him. I took the phone, watching Bryan and Dad head to the kitchen. He was going to help Dad prepare his meal.

"Hey honey, how's it going?" a voice asked from the other end of the call.

"Mum?"

"Of course it's Mum. How are you, baby?"

"I'm fine," I said grumpily. "How's work?"

"It's just terrible here, honey. How about you, did you get any work done at school today?"

"Yeah. Yeah, sure."

The line went silent for a while and I said nothing, the call filling up with the sound of my breathing.

"Is something wrong?"

"What? Nothing," I said, willing myself to talk normally.

"Ryan? I'm your mother, I carried you boys for nine months; I can tell when you're hurting. Tell me, baby, what is going on?"

I exhaled, watching Dad trudge back to his room to change into some clean clothes while Bryan set the table.

"What's wrong, baby? Did you get into a fight at school today?"

"No."

"How about your assignments? Are you in trouble with some—?"

"It's nothing, Mum."

"So you did get into trouble regarding assignments…"

"What? No," I coughed as my brother returned, wearing that asking look about how things were going on the phone. I shook my head and lowered my eyes. *Bad.*

"Then what is it, Ryan?"

I went quiet again.

"Nothing. Just a bad mood. I'll be alright."

"Alright baby, is your brother there?"

I handed Bryan the phone, hurrying to the fridge to grab a bottle of water. Dad was on his way back now, looking relaxed in that top and shorts he wore so often. I set the glass of crisp, cold before my old man and returned to the couch, still in silence. Our old man turned the TV on, its static noise quickly filling the house, and I grumbled quietly as I rose from the couch and made to leave.

"Where are you going?" Dad called as I trudged off.

"My room." It was more of our room, Brian's and mine, but I wasn't in for possessive pronouns at the moment. I just wanted to get to bed.

"You don't want to see this with me?" he said, nodding at the screen, where a series was running. We all watched it together from time to time but tonight, I just found the whole idea of staring at a picture box nauseating. I shook my head and waved goodnight as I continued to the bedroom. I was lying down only a few minutes, my eyes still wide open, staring at the bunk bed above me when the door slowly creaked opened. Bryan's light steps moved in, and telling from how gentle they were, he was up to no good.

"Not tonight, Bry," I blurted before twisting and turning. He stopped and smiled, sinking down next to me.

"You look terrible."

"We're twins, remember," I said.

"Why didn't you tell her what was going on?"

"Tell her what?"

"About, you know, it."

I glared up at my brother, raising a brow. "What are you talking about?"

I knew what he was talking about: the election and how we didn't have any direction regarding the campaign, but I wasn't in any sort of mood to talk about it, not with Mum at least.

"I have no idea what you're talking about, Bryan," I said, my head resting on the soft blue sheets of my bed.

Bryan sighed as he laid down next to me, both of us now looking at the bunk above us.

"Dad still watching his show?"

"Nope," Bryan said. "He's on the phone again. Mum."

"She's still on?" I said, surprised.

"What does it sound like?" Bryan sighed. "Told her about the election."

"Oh, okay. Cool," I said, disinterested.

Smack!

"Ugh!" I groaned. He had hit me in the face with a pillow. I glared at him, cold-eyed, calculating my retaliation. "What did you do that for?"

"Nothing. Just felt like it."

I climbed up, reaching for the pillow on the bunk above when we heard Dad call both our middle names from the kitchen. Bryan and I locked eyes, on the same team once more. This couldn't be good, I thought. Usually, Dad liked to visit our room whenever he had something to say to us. However, he only called us down if we were in some sort of trouble. What could Mum have said to him on that call?

"We better hurry," Bryan said, already heading for the door. I rose, staring at my feet as I walked to my doom.

I got down to the living room and found Bryan seated on the couch opposite Dad. Dad still had his eyes on the TV, the series gradually wrapping up. It seemed we would have to wait for our destruction.

"Sit next to your brother, Ken," he said, never looking away from the TV. I strode towards Bryan, my eyes on Dad.

"What happened?" I whispered to Bryan, but he wouldn't budge. He just sat, seemingly content to remain silent. Dad turned off the TV finally, his eyes coming to rest on mine.

"So, what's going on at school?" Dad said, his baritone voice echoing off the walls. The air grew thick as silence polluted the normally lively room, the background humming of the TV now a long and loud nothingness screaming at the back of my skull.

"Nothing, why do you ask?" Bryan said, his hands knotting into fists.

"Kenneth, is that so?" he said, looking to me once more.

I fell quiet, swallowing. "We didn't fight anybody, Dad."

A few weeks back, another kid had been bothering me at school. I told Bryan about it and together, we had confronted him. Bryan knew everything about faking confidence and using the kind of language to scare people, so when we approached the kid, I vanished while Bryan handled the confrontation. Eventually, the kid started talking back and tried to punch Bryan. Bry smacked him, sending him sprawling backward so that he fell, landing hard on his back.

The kid was even angrier when he stood, and Bryan kept asking him to stop, saying that he didn't want to hurt anyone, that he just wanted the kid to leave me alone, but before Bryan could finish those words, the kid reared back and kicked him in the groin. I groaned in pain from where I was perched. Sensing my brother's agony, I lurched towards the kid, smacking him from behind. Unfortunately, it was at that moment that one of the teachers spotted us, and when our opponent saw the teacher, he started weeping, saying we had attacked him first. It was a serious situation and it nearly got us suspended. Dad was asked to visit the school and when he got home, we heard the sermon of our lives.

Bryan and I stared at our dad, afraid of another sermon, or worse. Mr. Willie Wood wouldn't quit watching us with those hazel eyes, his jaw so finely arched that it looked like he wore Hollywood makeup. He cleared his throat, a sound we associated with moments when he had something serious to talk about.

"Your mother told me you're running for president."

I watched a smile creep back into Bryan's face. Words were coming back to him as our fear began to subside.

"Yes," Bryan said, twiddling his fingers in a nervousness that was now rooted in excitement instead of dread.

"So, how's that going?" Dad said. I could tell he was happy about it, although he had a way of trying to mask it. There was a slight dose of enthusiasm in his voice. What really gave it away, though, were his hazel eyes that now seemed to have lit up. I stifled a smile as my breaths came easier.

"Not good," Bryan admitted, still finding it a little hard to discuss his struggles with Mr. Willie Wood. "We're still trying to get kids to join us."

"Not sure they'd want to join two boys who nearly beat up a kid a couple weeks ago, right?" he said.

Bryan cocked his head with shame, his eyes glued to his feet. "Right."

"Just as I thought," Dad said, adjusting so that he sat at the edge of his seat, a smile finding its way across his face. "So, let's hear your plan."

Bryan looked over to me, then back to our father. "We…have no plan."

"Is that right?" Dad said, his gaze sliding in my direction.

I nodded, eyes down.

Dad ran his palms over his head as he reclined into the couch, amusement still evident in his expression. "Sounds like you boys have a lot to learn about blindly jumping into stuff. Tell me, Keith, why are you doing this again?"

"Umm...I—"

"You just lost an election," Dad said. "I just asked you a vital question and you're stuttering. A moment like that costs you the election. Listen son, and Ken, you should hear this too; you can't be stuttering when someone asks you a question. You can't. You have to be prepared for the worst. You have to study and prepare with the idea that all these kids hate your guts and just want to embarrass you. That's how hard you have to try."

Bryan wiped his face with his palms, both of which seemed to have sweat collecting on them. I exhaled where I sat, several questions popping in my head.

"To excel at anything, you have to know why you want do it. The world is crazy, boys. People are crazy. Not everyone has their lives figured out as much as they should. There is no blueprint on how to live a good life. Yes, the Bible gives us a decent idea and how to treat others, but there is no singular set of rules to life. Everyone is out there looking for meaning. People pray to God, Allah, Buddha, all these deities for a sense of direction...for order. So, boys, you have to know what you want and the direction you want to take. You can't do it blind."

"How…how can we win the election?" I asked, finally finding the courage to move my mouth.

"That's the wrong question," Dad said. "It's a self-centered question. Every candidate is thinking the same way. If you're going to make headway with this, you'll have to think differently than them. Stop asking how you can get what you want…and start asking your voters, the kids at school, what they want and how you can get it for them."

It clicked in that moment. It was all we needed to hear. Later that night, Bryan and I spent time considering what the kids found annoying, what we could introduce to spice up the whole experience of school. When we finally slept, we had tons of ideas that would never make it into our agenda, but there were a couple ideas that would fly. We woke up the next morning excited to put them to the test.

We left for school earlier than usual. Bryan and I had dug into our savings, taking a good sum with us. On our way to school, we headed into a store. We spent about twenty minutes there before racing over to the school.

By lunch, kids were passing my brother and me, all of them stopping to express their goodwill.

"Hey, Bryan," one of the kids said, "heard about this morning. That was sick."

"Yeah, can we get some?" another said, the two of them circling us like vultures.

"Nah, we're out of them. Tomorrow though, if you're lucky to make it early, you'll get some," I said, coolly.

"Awesome," the first of the boys said, running off with his friend. Before he left the cafeteria, he turned and called, "And good luck with the elections. If you don't win, then I don't know who will."

When they were gone, Bryan's face was aglow.

"See, it's working," I said.

"I don't know. We probably shouldn't get too excited about this," he said, the smile quickly evaporating after the compliment.

"Don't worry, bro. You've got this."

"You're just saying that because you're not the one running…"

"Hey, I didn't want to go into politics," I shot back, then regretting it immediately, I reached for his hand, tapping it as a group of girls walked past, smiling and waving at us after taking part in the morning's activities.

"It's a brilliant plan, Bryan. Everyone likes you already. I think it'll work."

"I don't even know if I want it anymore. It's just…"

"Scary?"

"More like…unsettling. It's like there's a third world war happening in my stomach, and in my head."

I chuckled, then stopped when I saw that he wasn't laughing along. He had a pained look on his face.

"What?" I said. "It's funny."

"To you, everything is funny," he said, looking down at the table. There was a piece of cardboard on the table staring back at him. The letters written on the cardboard spelled his name. A few smaller words just below mentioned the election. I watched him roll his eyes and plaster a fake smile on his face. I looked up to see more kids were heading for our table.

Earlier that morning, Bryan and I had stood right at the school gate just as it had opened. We had done this so we could welcome the kids ourselves and distribute our purchases from the store downtown.

Candy.

From the list of ideas, this one was Bryan's. He thought it would be great if we could find something that all the kids had a *thing* for. Although we initially feared that some of them would consider it a silly tactic for publicity, it worked well. The kids at Lord Baltimore Middle School were pleasantly surprised when they reached the school gate and met two boys handing out candy, a cardboard sign behind them declaring Bryan Wood a worthy presidential candidate.

The next day, we did it again. We left home early, visited the store, bought candy, and distributed it at the school gate. The fun part of this was that it encouraged kids to come to school early, and it encouraged those who may have been absent the day before to show up today. From every corner, you could spot them, kids from all over the neighborhood, pouring into the school gate, each of them getting candy while they high-fived the presidential candidate.

After our house management gigs that day, we set out to come up with a plan of action for when Bryan became elected. We also foresaw that we couldn't keep handing out candy for much longer. We needed to develop something that would captivate everyone. Something great. Having come up with a few ideas we thought wouldn't work, we decided to ask Dad for some wisdom.

"Candy every morning? Wow, I didn't think that was allowed," Dad said, amused.

"We haven't gotten in trouble, so far" I said.

"So far," Dad echoed.

I went quiet, while Bryan prepared to take notes in a small notebook.

"What problems do you think kids at school have? You have to convince them that you're going to solve their problems," Dad said.

"Ah, Dad, where to start? There's so much to do, so much that kids our age want," Bryan said, glancing up from his notes.

"Kids want good grades, easy classes; they hate math, and would kill to have thirty minutes of extra recess."

"Not everyone hates math," Bryan replied. I could see Dad smirking at our exchange.

"Actually, everyone does," I said, "at least the ones who are smart enough to admit it. Besides, didn't you say you hated math, that you just happen to be good at it?"

"No, I did not!" Bryan shot back, glancing meekly at Dad as if he had just used a swear word.

"Listen up," Dad said, "easy classes and skipping math isn't happening. But a longer recess, now that might be possible."

"So you're saying we can ask for those?" Bryan said.

"No," Dad retorted, "I'm saying you can tell the kids you'll help them fight for longer breaks if they elect you as president. You'll be their champion."

"Brilliant." I clapped my hands. "It'll drive them nuts."

Bryan was nodding now, apparently sold on the idea. Now that we knew our main message, we needed to polish our strategy. As I said before, we couldn't continue buying candy and handing it out. Our savings would dry up quickly. We decided to come up with something that would not cost us anything in terms of monetary value, but at the same time, it would have to be something the kids would find enjoyable and valuable.

We had thought about hosting a small promotional party at our place, but that wasn't happening. At least, not yet. We weren't old enough to host parties, and even if we were, it would cost us money and we were pretty serious about not touching our savings. The following day, we didn't hand out candy, and the reaction was immediate. The kids were heartbroken when they showed up at the school gate and found that we weren't there. Throughout the day, we were sent notes and confronted by many disappointed and angry potential voters. The recess break wasn't exactly any better. Bryan and I were constantly bombarded with questions that weren't exactly mean or rude, just innocent kids letting us know how they felt about their one supply of happiness being unceremoniously cut off.

Bryan kept a confident face and assured them that we had a new plan brewing and that they shouldn't fret. We didn't share candy for quite a while, and although this was going according to plan, we had our doubts. On the day before the election, Bryan had to give a speech. We knew our chances of getting booed off stage was pretty high, considering the lack of candy distribution.

We expected the kids would believe we were incompetent. However, what they didn't know was that for days, Bryan and I had been practicing a dance routine. While Dad helped Bryan polish his speech, us boys took the big stereo to our room and turned on the music. We came up with dance steps that were easy to learn but still looked good. We had secretly enlisted a few friends, too. We told them we had a surprise for the entire school and they could never tell anyone about it. Curiosity was piqued.

Bryan and I ached to tell them, to share our excitement, but based on Dad's instruction and advice, we didn't. All we told them was that they had a part to play for the upcoming election. We also promised them some goodies as long as they kept the secret. We also proposed our plans to the principal, and, lucky enough, Mum had come with us because Dad had been too busy. It was uncomfortable watching Mum and our principal go back and forth over the details of our plan. Eventually, when we were asked what kind of song we would be playing, it was a relief to know that we had chosen a song that wouldn't pose a problem for the school to play for its students. It was a smooth high-school song that didn't create any threat, so the principal gave us the go-ahead.

On election day, we said we would give our speech last, but that did not pan out, for some reason. Due to some strange twist of fate, Bryan was mysteriously called to give his speech first. I watched the principal's chair with cold feet, Bryan leaning forward to confirm that we had both heard correctly.

"You're up," one of the other candidates poked at Bry, sensing his unease at the mishap.

I turned to Bryan, my heart beating so fast that I was sure I would collapse at any moment.

"This will be great," I said, patting his shoulder. He rose unsteadily, quickly leafing through the pages he and Dad had come up with. As he trudged towards the stage, I felt a sudden urge to follow him, to support him. It was then I saw the principal having a pretty heated talk with the event organizer. Soon, I spotted the DJ running through his list of songs. Oh boy, I thought, quickly racing to the group of kids we had enlisted, alerting them to the change in plans. Without hesitation, they raced towards the lockers while I caught up with my brother.

"What're you doing?"

"Hold the notes, we're dancing….now," I said as we got on stage. Quickly, Bryan disposed of the notes just as the music started to turn up.

As, the music started and we started to make our moves, the kids were uncomfortably quiet. We feared they were going to boo us off the stage. It was only a matter of time, though, before the kids we'd enlisted started going up and down the rows of chairs, handing out candy. The kids went wild. This time, we had purchased higher quality candy than before, which had been wrapped in fine cardboard cut-outs with the words "Vote Bryan."

I felt relief wash through my lungs as I watched the kids react so positively. For a moment, we thought it was going to get too rowdy, but thankfully it didn't. The music stopped abruptly, and the organizer pushed Bryan quickly to his speech. The kids voiced their disapproval when this happened, all of them begging to have the performance continue, but it was to no avail. So, Bryan made his speech.

When Bryan was done, the entire school was cheering, including the principal. When we both returned to our seats, we got high-fives and compliments from all around us. Even the kids who had helped us out seemed impressed as they munched on what was left of the candy. When the other kids were done with their speeches, a chant began to rise from the students.

"We want Bryan! We want Bryan! We want Bryan!"

The organizers couldn't get them to stay quiet, so they called Bryan up to talk to them. Bryan went up and, holding the mic confidently, simply smiled and asked the kids what he could do to make them calm. One of the kids we enlisted yelled, "Teach us your dance moves," which elicited another cheer.

Soon, kids were pushing me towards the stage. The music had started again and we started to dance once more. We went over the steps together, teaching the students how to do the moves as they cheered and danced in place. On the day of the election, Bryan was declared the winner.

Rule 3

What the Market Wants

At the dawn of 2020, when the Coronavirus gradually began spreading, few ever considered how much of an impact it would have, and for how long. As lockdowns became a trend around the world, restaurants were shutting down and theme parks closed. The same could be said for regularly scheduled events that required people to gather en masse (religious institutions, schools, large offices, etc.).

The schools struggled mightily. For the few who had gone virtual, they kept up with their services—even though you and I know about the average student's attention issues based on a few viral videos of high school online classes gone wrong—while others who weren't smart and agile enough to keep up with the technological train were soon booted off the tracks, sent sprawling into the abyss of nonexistence, another victim of the pandemic's spread.

COVID brought to light a deep and ancient truth about the world we live in: Reality is unstable. The stock market rises and falls, businesses that seem to be doing fine suddenly go bankrupt, accidents happen with no prior warning, trains run out of track and derail. In short, nothing stays the same forever. Like COVID has taught us, there is no definite way to arm ourselves against the unforeseen forces that make up our reality. We can't fully predict what will happen, but we can be quick to react and exploit it. According to an article by Business Insider, Amazon founder Jeff Bezos made $48 billion (USD) during this pandemic (between March and June 2020). The same was also said of Elon Musk of Tesla, alongside others, who made about $185 billion (USD) and is now the richest man in the world.

The question is, how was it even possible that these guys made all this money during a recession? How does one reach their level, staying high and almost untouchable by unpredictable economic turns? These are questions that many have asked and are still asking. Well, we do not assume to be experts, but based on statistics, we have a clue—or something that looks pretty much like it—about how these guys keep doubling their profits at will. What follows is our wildest guess, or what I would call the closest thing to an explanation.

A company like Amazon has been refined to suit one particular need in our fast-paced, everyone-is-busy world: the ease of purchase. Of course, this isn't the only thing that makes Amazon stand out. Other things like their pricing, shipping costs, etc. are enough to woo most, but let's focus on that bit about ease. For a world as busy as ours, services requiring almost zero input from users are nearly impossible to spot. Say you wanted to get stuff at Walmart in the pre-pandemic world. What happens? You would usually spot lines at the cashier, or there's the trouble of having to drive down to the mall.

There's also the hassle of making sure you get there on time, because you need to be home quickly so you can help your six-year-old with her assignment because you couldn't help her with it during the week. This is because you get home from your nine-to-five job and you're too exhausted to even stare at your kid twice, let alone have a meaningful conversation with them.

Almost seventy percent of the population works at a job that requires they clock about nine hours of work per day. They are drones with specific duties and several leftover tasks from the previous day, always too much to get done in the time they are given. They are in a race against time and should they be unable to meet a given quota at the end of the month, it's goodbye. Now, think about how invaluable Amazon is to them. With a few clicks on your PC, you can expect to have your purchase delivered to you. No long lines, no trip to the store. Sandra gets her homework done. Daddy gets to sleep in peace. Everyone's happy.

Amazon didn't start as a company that sold such a wide range of products. It was more of an online bookstore at its beginnings. At the time, Mr. Bezos, who worked at a marketing firm, had seen how the market for the internet was growing exponentially. Spotting potential, he resigned from his marketing job, and, having invested all the money he could squeeze into his budding company, had his parents do the same. At the time, Amazon.com was the joke of the century. Who needs an online bookstore? What a total waste. Amazon[DOT]boom. On and on, tabloids blasted the company for its slow start and inevitable failure. During the era of the dotcom boom—the age when the internet exploded into a global, eye-catching vehicle—Amazon's value had gradually pivoted. Soon, Jeff figured, "Hey, we can do more than just sell books."

In an interview, when he was asked about the shift from purely book sales to what it is today, Jeff answered without a beat, "We had started wondering what we could do differently. We put out surveys, asking people what they would like us to offer…what products would they like to see…and the answers started trooping in. Most of them didn't know. Some listed things as silly as screwdrivers, while others said this and that. It was then we (Amazon) thought, 'we could sell literally anything.'"

For Jeff Bezos, he had to ask what the market desired. Although he didn't get a straight answer, he had enough insight to spot a distinct pattern amidst the tirades of seemingly unconnected responses. With his insight, he realized what the market needed was an online mall. Today, Jeff is the richest man in the world. This happens when you spot a want in the market, a specific 'something' that no other entrepreneur spots. It's not enough to just spot that need, though. You have to develop structures that meet those needs before someone else does.

Like Bryan's presidential campaign back at Lord Baltimore Middle School (though if you had asked us, we'd have had no idea that what we were up to was a campaign), we tuned in to what the kids wanted. We didn't just assume or guess. We didn't deliver a two-hundred-and-fifty-page book on how to be cool and be great at math and have the teachers love you so much that they slap your report cards with A's (which wouldn't be a bad idea for a book, except that no middle school kid would sit to read through a two-hundred-and-fifty-page book written by twin boys, one of whom hated math). That's just an extreme approach, and you can assume we would have lost the election way before any kid reached page twenty.

Instead, we focused on their immediate needs, things we could impact. They weren't necessarily bothered about their grades. Instead, they wanted things that made them happy. School was mostly dense, boring and filled with long, hellish moments of staring at a teacher that relentlessly spit out gibberish that they would fail to remember at the end of the term. While most students came from average families, candy probably wasn't something a lot of their parents encouraged too often, especially in the mornings. It was these issues that we tackled with our campaign. We struck where it mattered the most: those unspoken needs that ached their small bodies. We gave out candy. Bryan's speech promised longer recess break hours and finally, we entertained them with a fun dance. We won their hearts.

A two thousand and x research carried out by x and y says that x company will be out of business in the next two to four years. Why? Because they are too focused on a niche that is fast becoming non-existent, obsolete. Jobs requiring tons of paperwork will be taken over by AI. Secretaries, waiters, and waitresses, butlers, chauffeurs, these jobs will be non-existent. Why will this happen? Did people get tired of needing such services? No, but someone smart enough to develop systems and machines that carry out these tasks faster and cheaper, requiring as little effort as possible on the part of their potential customers, will be throwing the old-fashioned guys out of business without a second thought. Evolve or die, baby!

How to Print Your Own Money

One exciting field trip we could never forget was to Washington D.C's Bureau of Engraving and Printing. During the tour, we were wowed by the large printing machines, especially the ones that printed sheets of fresh U.S. currency. The chiming of the machines followed by how they ran along multiple spots to get slapped with differing inks was such a joy to witness.

For most of us, there is no large estate we will be inheriting from anyone. No company document will have our name under the title of "Owner." Most of you will be starting the game from scratch, building from nothing to something. This is because you don't have the leverage that the top one percent has; you guys will be printing your own new money—from the bottom up. No genie popping from anywhere to grant you three wishes. Just the pure grind of hard work. This was how it was for us. We had watched our parents work at jobs they didn't particularly like in exchange for stability. These jobs took a chunk of time from their lives every day and gave them some money and benefits at the end of the month. This wasn't the kind of system we wanted to enter. We wanted to be rich with money and time. We wanted to be rich and young. Young enough to enjoy the wealth we would accumulate and not putting around in a Porsche in our late sixties when reaching the speed limit itself might kill us.

1. A Reason Worth Printing For

Finding a side hustle while in middle school really worked for us because we were sensitive to societal pressures. Being two young black kids who stuck around each other for quite a while didn't particularly win us the fame we wanted from the world around us. Although we would eventually find a way to exploit this habit of always being together, we suffered a good deal of backlash from outsiders. We weren't cool enough, they said. We wore the same baggy clothes, had the same school accessories and almost had the same handwriting. We could never fit into their clique. But that wasn't going to hurt as much as being rejected by girls.

Yes, girls.

We had more than our share of ordeals with them. What we failed to mention earlier was that it was actually a rejection that had struck us so hard and made us want to be liked and popular at school. Before the whole side hustle thing, we were just two middle school kids, wearing matching clothes, doing things together without any other care or concern. We thought we were pretty cool and that everyone would like us. We quickly discovered the error in our logic.

We were boring, apparently. We never could spend time around other kids without our twin. I guess we had learned to be so co-dependent over the years that it was difficult to be a normal kid without the other. When I was left with other kids and my brother wasn't around, I would usually unconsciously talk about my brother and all of the great things he did, to which the other kids would roll their eyes. My brother experienced the same thing. Initially, we thought they were just being mean. Our idea of 'cool' was just so warped that it would take some serious heartbreak to knock some sense into us. Sometimes pain can drive you to change.

Bryan was smart enough to catch the funny looks he got every time he tried to bring me up during chats with the other kids. He used to talk about how he enjoyed spending time with me and how there were a lot of cool aspects of having a twin. It was something we unknowingly rubbed in people's faces when we brought it up. We didn't consider that others could not experience it. Well, as you would guess, it was only natural that they hated our guts.

Soon, Bryan stopped talking about me, as he responded to the social cues he was receiving. The kids, knowing our habit of always saying nice things about each other, started picking on him and teasing him by asking him what nice thing I had done for his precious twin that week. He used to think they were really interested, and he went over long details of the fun times we had together. When he caught on to what they were really doing, though, he stopped. Whenever he was asked from then on, he would say nothing. However, there was one instance when he decided to say something. A girl he liked had been part of their group and they had all been talking quite alright until one of the kids, a bully, asked him what fun little adventures he had with me that week.

"Well, nothing particularly fun," Bryan had said. "It's funny, thinking being a twin is fun, until your twin wets the bed and you get blamed."

The kids had laughed, patting him on the shoulder as he had redirected the focus away from him. That was a good one, they said, going further to ask whether I (Ryan) had really peed my pants. Sensing the pressure and a chance at being liked, he nodded and they laughed harder. Even the girl laughed. He felt good knowing he was now in their clique. Or so he thought.

Word quickly got out that I had apparently wet my pants. Walking through the hallways, kids were approaching me to ask if I'd actually peed myself. I remember running off to the bathroom after a few students had begun to point and laugh. I cried, wondering why this rumor had started. I didn't know about the joke, and worse, I didn't know my brother had told it. I wouldn't know until the next day I found Bryan crying in the bathroom, just as I had the day before.

"What happened?" It was break time, and I had suddenly started feeling down after taking a language test that I was so sure I'd passed. I wasn't sure why I felt that way until I spotted my brother weeping. If you recall, Bryan and I share a connection. We mirror each other's feelings. It's like we have this telepathic ability to experience any extreme emotions that the other has.

Bryan wiped his face. "It's nothing." A short pause. "I asked a girl out, and she turned me down."

"Well, it's really nothing to cry over," I said. "I guess she's just not good enough for my twin."

"It's easy for you to say when it's not you who got embarrassed."

Bryan would later reveal that the girl had rejected him out loud in the cafeteria where the other kids could hear.

"She said…she can't be with someone whose brother pees his pants."

Those words hit me, and I recall feeling my knees tremble.

"But that's not true," I said. "I don't pee my pants." It was the rumor, but who started it?

Bryan looked up, my eyes now moist, mirroring his.

"I'm sorry, Ry," he said. "It was just a stupid joke. It was…me."

He explained how the joke had originated. Furious, I didn't speak to him for the rest of that day. When we got home, he fell ill. Later that night, I too had fallen ill.

2. The Better Plan

The old fashioned 'get a job, start saving early so you can retire at 65 and have a lot of cash' is just a sloppy route to success in today's economy. It's a decent plan, but if you plan to make a ton of money, then that plan is a long shot. Take a look around you. Observe everyone who followed the old fashioned plan of 'go to school, get a job.' Are they really wealthy? The Ph.D., all those certificates they accumulated; what do they get in return for that? Longer work hours? A more specific field of work that reduces their usefulness in another field if there's ever a meltdown that wipes out the significance of their current field? And they get very few raises over the course of a career, say about 15-20 percent increase in their income. Is that your path to get wealthy, by exchanging all of your time for money until you hardly have enough time for yourself and your family, all while the money you're earning isn't as much as you'd hoped?

This plan is flawed, especially today. It was something we learned right around the time Bryan and I started our candy business. It was while Bryan and I had fallen ill after our confrontation in the school bathroom over the peeing joke. Of course, Mum thought it was just a regular fever that had hit us both. She had no idea it was the twin connection that had brought about the whole illness. In a week, we would be up and kicking again, both of us warily walking by the many kids staring daggers at us in the hallways. It's a wonder we managed to pull through, emotionally. It was a few days later that Bryan and I would make our request to Mum for the five hundred bucks so we could upgrade our wardrobe and show those kids just how it's done, but you know how that turned out already.

On that night following the talk with Mum, Dad had returned home late as usual and, after he was done with dinner and relaxing on the big couch while Mum snuggled with him, she told him about the talk we'd had. Moments later, we heard a knock on our door.

"It's Dad," the voice said as it creaked open. His head poked through the doorway, an exhausted yet hopeful smile on his face. "Can I come in?"

Of course he could. Bryan and I sat up as he walked in, something we usually did as a gesture of respect, but he told us to stay seated as he dragged a chair close to us.

"Mum's told you, hasn't she?" Bryan said, his eyes glued to his feet. Dad laughed.

"What do you two boys need five hundred bucks for?"

"We don't need it anymore," I said.

"Yeah, she told me that, too. Just curious, though. Wanted to hear it for myself," he said.

There was a brief moment of silence and I could hear the tension stretch in the air. Although there actually was no tension, I still felt a bit uncomfortable every time Dad was acting so freely with us. He wasn't overbearing in any way, but he was strict. He, like Mum, detested lying and wanted to see us looking sharp. He didn't want for us the kind of childhood he had growing up.

"It's a good thing, what you boys have decided to do. I'm proud of you both."

I was unsure of whether I had heard him correctly. I did notice that Bryan smiled. I must have, too, but I don't know when the smile appeared on my face.

"You know, there's a lot to life that school can't prepare you for," Dad said as he rubbed his tired eyes. "There's just way too much, and I should say, whatever venture you have in mind is a great starting point. I have no doubt you boys will go on to make some money. But, for now, you should get some sleep," he said, rising to leave.

"I thought going to school was important," I said as he reached the door.

"Of course, it is. Very. Sometimes, though, what you learn at school can be harmful to your growth. School teaches you a few paths, but not all of them."

Right there, I could feel a question mark hovering over my head, almost the opposite of a light bulb that would signify an idea. What was Dad talking about?

"You know, I went through a lot when I was your age. Paid my way through school, hoping it would grant me everything I ever wanted. Well, it didn't exactly grant me everything," Dad said, heading back to where he had been sitting. "Look, school prepares you for a job and following orders all your life, maybe with a chance to give some orders after several years. I don't want my kids growing into another couple of certificate holders who will find a spot in the job market. Billionaires, boys. You're going to grow into billionaires, and that doesn't happen through a salary."

At this point, we had totally lost any grasp of what he was saying. Mr. Willie Wood said it was okay, that we would understand when we got older.

As we graduated high school, those wise sayings came back to us. While others went on to look for jobs while awaiting the transition to college, Bryan and I had saved a lot and were on the lookout for a worthwhile adventure. We feared the possibility that we might end up as bums, but our desire to gain wealth remained unshakeable, and, based on our evaluations at the time, we found Dad's words to be true: no billionaire got there with a salary.

We saw that our teachers at school, the attendants at the store downtown, and even the security guy who worked at one of the houses we managed—all of them had attended college, some were even Master's degree holders. The reality hit us hard, and we knew that the plan of college and a job was rigged against building wealth. There was something the ultra-wealthy knew that we didn't, and we made it our task to figure out what it was. What we lacked in knowledge, we would make up for in pure grit and commitment.

3. Success Garage

We were lucky enough to figure out quite early that the good old mantra of 'go to school, get a job and save' wasn't going to cut it if we were ever going to live our dream lives. After high school, we took a break from all the houses we managed. It was time for another brainstorming session, but we weren't kids anymore. We wanted to plan out our future. We had to.

We considered it an incubation period. It was during this time that Bryan and I came up with the name 'New Money Twinz.' We planned to print our own currency (literally) and hand it out to people we met during a long road trip that would take us into the world. We also started writing songs, a messy process that made us feel a bit like bums. The good thing was that there was a lot of data to back up the reality that we were on the right path, even though we were in the early stages. Although we had no solid tertiary education at the time, we had heard of stories of Steve Jobs and Steve Wozniak, who started Apple in a garage, and that of Google founders Larry Page and Sergi Grin. We were going to make it big, we thought, so we decided to jump on the rebellious train and go against every social convention towards genuine wealth, especially the ones we knew to be untrue.

In the year 2000, Bryan and I, now nineteen, moved to California and never looked back. At that time, we had about $4000 in cash, all saved up from the housing gigs we had. We set out into the world, taking nothing from our mum and dad except for the several years of advice and guidance they had provided to us, things we would find to be of no small value to our journey.

Honestly, we weren't certain about what we were doing. We just knew we had to leave home, broaden our experiences. I guess we wanted to explore, to see all there was to the world. We lived on the road, benefitting from the many kind gestures of people we encountered along the way. We were traveling blind, and all we knew was that we wanted to be rich. We slept in cars, houses and sometimes hotels. One of the best memories we have was when we stayed in the garage of one of our many benefactors we encountered on our journey.

It was an interracial couple. The husband was black, and his wife was a Canadian American. They had shown us love in their small apartment, allowing us to sleep on their couch. For the sake of anonymity, we will call them the Damians. Mr. Damian had a garage where he parked an old Mustang. He had shown it to Bryan and me on our third night with them. Its engine was long dead and yet, he kept the car clean. Mr. Damian was that kind of man. He even let us climb in, telling us stories of his youth as we looked in wonder at the vehicle.

They didn't have kids, so we guess it was only natural that he enjoyed interacting with two young men that could have been his own sons in another life. As the days went by, Bryan and I often sat in the Mustang, dreaming about our future. The garage became our office for those few weeks, and the Mustang a vehicle for catapulting us into a future where we had accomplished everything we had ever dreamed. There, we were able to better sculpt our desires and the plans to back them up. By day we would help the Damians at home and, having had a long nap, by night Bryan and I were either writing songs or perfecting some fresh dance moves. A few concerts were coming up and we sought to earn a spot in them. Remember, we were starting fresh, and in a new place. We had no contacts in high places, no manager to assist with the responsibility of finding shows for us. All we had was ourselves.

One afternoon, Bryan was watching a television show on the WB Network called the Ricki Lake Show. On the show, they were advertising a slot for something called 'siblings players,' an avenue for siblings to showcase their talents. Bryan was beyond ecstatic as he scribbled down the hotline number for participants to call. He quickly dialed the number and left a message. Surprisingly, we got a call back! They wanted us on the show. The excitement we felt was palpable.

4. It's the Fulfilment, Not the Money

We rehearsed and wrote songs and raps the entire time we were in California and, well, it began to pay off. Staying at the garage had forced us to hone our skills. For most young people out there, they usually wait for the opportunity to present itself before they make the necessary improvements or acquire the right skill, or do whatever they should do for the opportunity. But this is having it all backwards. Unless you've made a name for yourself, it's nearly impossible to deliver what you cannot prove to be capable of, or do not already have. Just imagine if we had sat at home, twiddling our thumbs, gaining no skill or talent. We would have never had our eyes out for shows like that, and even if we had, we would be entirely unprepared and unqualified. There's a saying: good luck is when skill meets opportunity. We don't ascribe to aspirational quotes, but that moment was a stroke of good luck for us. It was one of the pivotal moments that would catapult us into the future we had always dreamt of.

Being smart enough to position oneself for an opportunity is the very quality that separates the top one percent from the majority of individuals wallowing in poverty. The majority maintains the mindset of, 'I'll get ready when it comes,' but the top one percent thinks differently. They think: 'Unless I'm ready now, I can't seize the opportunity should it show up,' and hence, they strive to fashion themselves and their skills for such privileges way before the situations make use of those skills.

Remember what we said about entrepreneurs like Jeff Bezos and preparation? For us, besides the fact that we really wanted to make money, we were dedicated by our love for what we were doing. Dancing and rapping have always been activities we've found mesmerizing. It was always about the freedom to pursue whatever made us truly happy and provided a sense of accomplishment, which was to entertain. I think the seed for this mindset started budding after we saw how our classmates in middle school reacted to our performance during the presidential speech. It felt so good, to be accepted and appreciated by so many in that moment. The response we received following the event rippled throughout the area. We liked that. The fact that we made people feel that way was fulfilling. This is why we decided to go into entertainment.

This is the same path that any entrepreneur that is worth his salt must tread. You must find a big need that utilizes your skills. A need that you're excited to solve. It's more than just the money. Look, if you're doing it for money alone, chances are that you'll feel miserable for most of it, and you'll end up burnt out and hate yourself for it.

Mistakes are Lessons, but Don't Make Them Twice

At about age eighteen, our parents helped us purchase a used blue 1990 Toyota Corolla, and we were so pumped up about it. Although part of the money had come from our savings, it still felt good knowing we had purchased something so major. One night, I had stayed home while Bryan drove uptown to see a girlfriend. After leaving her house and driving through the city, he approached an intersection when the car's brakes failed and out of nowhere, was run into by another vehicle.

Bryan was knocked unconscious when his forehead smacked into the door window. His driver's side door caved from the impact. I was home watching a show when I felt an uncomfortably warm sensation suddenly clamp hard against my entire body. I fell to the floor, paralyzed. I could feel Bryan telepathically, the physical agony coursing through his body. It felt like we were talking through our minds, describing to each other what had just happened. He told me he had lost blood. Just then, the phone rang. When I finally managed to pick it up, the officer on the phone declared, "Your brother was just in a car crash." I screamed. Mum and

Dad heard me and we all hurried into Dad's truck for the hospital.

He was in fair condition when we reached the hospital. His forehead was badly bruised, but thank goodness, angels had protected him from worse. That day, we decided we would never buy second-hand stuff that had a chance of causing us harm.

As entrepreneurs, it's normal to want to cut costs and purchase products with slightly lower standards. It may be to save money or because you cannot afford the higher cost item. Nothing is as important as your life, though. If you're buying a vehicle that has issues and can take your life out of a mishap, then the money you were trying to save will end up in someone else's hands. As Mum said, money just sitting has no value. Be wise about your life. You deserve better. Your business deserves better and so do your dreams. Stop bootstrapping if your health is the cost. Remember, it's about having quality of life and fulfillment, not the money.

Back in California, we wanted to try out relationships. While we had had a few relationships throughout high school, it was never anything that lasted long, and we were often to blame. There were plenty of girls that wanted us, at least that was what we thought. There were a few, though. The issue was that when they found out about each other, it ended in a catfight, and soon Bryan and I just decided it was best we stopped. However, during our trip to California, we really considered the chances of us meeting our eventual spouses. Bryan and I always thought that we would have to date twins. It seemed, at the time, that it would make our journey and lifestyle less complicated and more fitting of a storybook. But would it?

After our road trips, we did end up meeting a set of twins. For the sake of anonymity, we'll call them Alice and Leisha. These girls were pretty, black American girls in their late teens. Although we were believers, we were still young men battling with the temptations that came with being flesh and blood. We had desires. Having gone out on a date with both girls, Bryan and I got different hotel rooms and thought we were going to make out, perhaps more.

Well, minutes into the date, I came out to use the bathroom. While I was in there, I spotted my brother walking into the restroom. Surprised, we laughed and both asked the other how the night was going. It turned out we would not be making love with either of the girls, as they had both started their menstrual cycle that night. That is the short version of how our dreams of twin relationships died.

Now, that experience wasn't a mistake. It was just one of those rare occurrences that confirmed our need to reconsider our conceptions of what a good life actually was. It's usually great to test things out to observe their practicality and dispel the aura. One of the not so amazing things about school is that we're loaded up with theories and tall tales, all of which don't necessarily have real-world applications. Entrepreneurs are risk-takers by nature. They can't afford to shy away from the likely inevitable doom of whatever they create or have in mind, because reward doesn't come without risk.

With this sense of practicality and risk-taking, they become acquainted with failure, their skins growing thick, thereby allowing them to test out ideas that will rock the world without getting their world rocked beyond repair. Guys like Jeff Bezos, Elon Musk, Michael Jordan, Oprah Winfrey, and others didn't sit idly and consider how cool it would be to do what they do now. No! They went out there and tried, and failed, and kept trying over and over until it all paid off. The path to financial freedom and fulfillment is a highway riddled with failures, and it takes a monstrous amount of courage and a failure-proof mindset to continuously move forward. To get comfortable with failure is to know true growth.

WHAT THEY DON'T TEACH YOU AT SCHOOL

Can you think for yourself?

During our senior year in high school, around Christmas, and Bryan and I were thinking of spending some good money. We had saved up a lot of cash and wanted to host a few friends over at our place. Our parents weren't going to be home so we thought we'd throw a party. At this time, we had become pretty popular at school and had strings of girlfriends whom, by the way, we'd hoped would never find out about each other. Teenage girls can be really mean to each other when they find out someone else is also into their boyfriend.

Eventually, the kids started showing up. Lots of them. There had been three girls who were into Bryan and two others who thought I were cute. We knew trouble was inevitable when they all showed up. We had each invited just one of the girls we were into, but, due to some sick twist of fate, the others had caught wind of the party and shown up.

Bryan and I went into hiding when we realized what had happened. We knew things would turn out for the worst if any of the girls spotted us. Luckily, we had left a few friends in charge of the drinks and party arrangements, so we didn't have to stick around to manage our own party. Bryan and I were tucked away in our room, peeking downstairs while a friend of ours, Borden, made trips up and down what was up with the girls and report back. Surprisingly, there wasn't much to fear at first. They all seemed to be doing just fine, until everyone kept wondering where we were.

Oh no.

"How long are you going to keep hiding?" Borden finally came to ask us. Bryan was by the window, his eyes on the street. He had a funny feeling our parents would arrive at any moment. Guilt can do that to you.

"You guys need to come up with a plan, and quick," Borden said. "This is getting tiring."

"Can't you take them out or something?" I asked.

"What? All two of them?"

"Five," Bryan said, turning to us. "There are five. Two into Ryan, three into me."

"Oh, and is that supposed to make it easier?" Borden said as he sank into the bed, throwing his head backward against the pillows. He was just as fed up as we were.

"Why did you even have to date all of them?" Borden said.

"It just happened. Besides," I shrugged, "what do you care?"

"It's just funny," Borden said, massaging his head.

"What is?"

"Having a lot of girls like you, and still having a hard time mixing with all of them. What are you, a polygamist?"

"You don't have to be such a jerk about it. We all know why no girl will even come close to kissing you," Bryan said.

In that instance, I saw the immediate regret in his eyes. Borden's eyes went wide, and the color drained out of his face. For a moment, I thought he would get up and run downstairs, maybe slam the door on his way out. He didn't, though. He just sat there, his eyes glittering back at us like a wounded puppy. It had not occurred to me at the time that he didn't have a girlfriend.

"I'm sorry, he didn't mean that," I said quickly.

Borden sighed, shaking his head. "It's alright. I'll go see what's going on, I guess."

"You aren't leaving, are you?"

He shook his head. "No, why would I leave—"

"Don't go, Borden," I said, hurrying towards the door so I could block it. "You don't have to."

Things went quiet for a while before Bryan spoke again.

"I'm sorry I said those words," Bryan said.

"You know, I never thought you would ever have so many girlfriends," Borden said, smirking. "You just didn't look like you would care about that stuff."

"We don't always care," I said.

"Then why are you tucked away in your room, running from *them*?"

I shrugged. "I don't know—"

"What's wrong with having girlfriends?" Bryan cut in.

"Nothing. The idea just never really appealed to me, and I thought we were alike."

"Haha, Borden, don't try to sound modest here. We all know you have a hard time getting girls to like you."

The smirk grew across Borden's face and for a moment, I thought it was the most sinister smile I had ever seen. He walked towards Bryan and I felt my heart jump, thinking for a second that he could actually push

Bryan out the window. But of course, that never happened.

"I do like girls and I find them attractive," Borden said, "but I find them annoying to keep up with, so I just gave up trying to pretend to be someone I'm not, especially since I was doing it for someone else."

"What do you mean?" I said.

"I realized having a girlfriend wasn't something that would benefit me in the long term."

"How can you think that way?" I said. "Everyone wants a girlfriend. It's a cool part of life."

Borden shook his head. "I never thought I would have to explain this to you guys, but you've got to learn to think for yourselves."

"Uh?" I raised a brow, stealing a glance at my brother, whose face was just as blank as mine.

"What are you even talking about?" I asked.

"Do you remember that one time when you guys swapped places…I mean on the team."

We both remembered, as it had not been long ago. We were on the baseball team at the time. Bryan always played the outfield and had gradually been bored out of his mind. After a long discussion, we reached an agreement to swap positions. However, I was the pitcher. So when he stepped in to pitch, the result was a disaster. Horrible. His play was so bad that it cost us the game. When the coach found out, he was pretty angry. He exploded at us, and for a moment, we feared we would be kicked off the team. We weren't, but we did sit out a few games. We never repeated such a selfish mistake.

That wasn't the only time we had switched, though. As I explained earlier, Bryan was pretty good with math and me, languages. There was a time during tests when we swapped seats. I took his language test while he took my math. Although things almost went wrong when a classmate of ours—some kid in our neighborhood who could tell us apart—had found out and threatened to tell the whole school. She told the teacher and to our relief, the teacher didn't believe her. It was a pretty close call though, one that would make us try to behave ourselves for the rest of our time in school.

"What has that got to do with this?" I asked Borden.

"At the game, when you switched places, that was the first time I saw you guys think for yourselves. You took advantage of the fact that you were twins. Smart thinking, that was."

"I still don't get it," I said, unsure of how to respond to the compliment. I understood, but I wasn't sure how to react. Or maybe I did and was too embarrassed about the whole thing. We had lost that game because of our stupid impulse and now, here was Borden, praising us for it.

"Never mind, you'll get it someday, hopefully," Borden said as he made his way out of the room. "There's noise downstairs and I can only hope it's not your girls causing a fight."

We risked a look downstairs and found the kids were really having a great time, but a small fraction of them were in a heated exchange. It was a boy and two of the girls I liked. I cringed when I saw their faces.

"What do we do, man?" I looked at Bryan.

"Don't ask me, they aren't my girlfriends," Bryan said nervously, shrugging.

Borden's words would echo through our entire lives, and now that I reflect on it, we have been thinking for ourselves for quite a long time. It never really occurred to us that way, though. Remember when we wanted to be cool at school and asked our mum for some cash? It was a blessing that she never gave it to us. It was just the right trigger we needed to think for ourselves, to ascend the social expectations. As I think about all those hours we spent trying to earn money, I feel a rush of adrenaline and happiness. Those were pretty amazing times, even if we didn't exactly feel that way while we were at it. Looking back now, we feel good because we know that we were building something. Not for anyone else, but for ourselves. We wanted to make some cash and we actually sat down to make it happen.

Many still hold the preconceived belief that going to school will sort you out for life, that it's the best path forward. While there is some speck of truth in those words, statistics show that millions and millions of graduates with various certificates have no solid job and are almost as useless as a broken door. Now, we do not mean to be harsh or overgeneralizing. This is not us saying you can never amount to anything because you are a graduate or are choosing the school route. Far from it. Bryan and I have benefited greatly thanks to the several courses we took, and you really should know that we are making a ton of money thanks to those courses. What we are really saying here is this: never assume that school has you covered, or is a free pass to success. Below are some of the fantastic advantages that come with going to a college or acquiring some sort of tertiary learning:

1. You get certified for the knowledge you have acquired.
2. You improve your connections thanks to the rapport you build with classmates, professors,

and the several other fellowships you will commit to in the course of your study.
3. You get a slight taste of what it feels like to be independent.
4. You increase your chance of being scouted by top companies.

The above are a few amongst the several benefits that come with acquiring tertiary knowledge. Please, if you can afford it, you should attend college or at least enroll in a scholastic program of some kind. Now, you may be wondering: What are you saying? One moment you're asking us to quit college, the next you are rooting for it!

Relax, and pay close attention.

College isn't bad and we aren't asking you to go or not to go. Instead, we implore you to dispose of the mindset that the mere act of attending college makes entitles you to some degree of business success. Although attending college increases your chances of success, the act by itself does not necessitate success. Have a look at the statistics on unemployed graduates and see what they say.

Why Entrepreneurs Fail

Right about the time we started our candy business back in Maryland, we foresaw making strong profits. We knew the kids in the neighborhood would want some. And yes, as we explained, we sold a good amount in the first few weeks of our endeavor. But over time, sales declined. We didn't take it well, at first. We were doing something wrong, and didn't know what it was. A brief talk with Mum would reveal the answer and how we could make corrections.

"You are selling to the wrong audience," Mum said.

"What do you mean? Everybody loves candy," I said, frowning.

"Yes, but have you asked who needs candy more, adults or kids?"

"Kids," I said, looking to Bryan, who was curled in Mum's lap. "Kids like candy more than adults."

"But who has more money to spend on purchases, kids or adults?"

"Adults," I said, not understanding.

"You see?" Mum said.

"But it doesn't sense. The rich kids have a lot of money to spend too," Bryan said, sitting up.

"Yes, that's true. Except that the overall population of rich kids around here, or anywhere, isn't exactly high. If you're going to start a business to sell candy to a few rich kids, I must say, you should be prepared to go broke before the end of the season when the stores are stocked with candy of higher quality that you cannot afford to purchase, let alone resell to someone who could just buy it themselves."

I remember sitting there, blinking for a moment as I tried to catch up with what Mum had just revealed to us.

"I never thought of that," I gasped.

It was true. Only adults had the extra money to buy candy, and yet, they didn't really want candy.

"What would you want, Mum?" I asked. "What would you pay good money for?"

"Definitely not shoes," Bryan laughed. "You have a lot of them already."

We all laughed.

"Anything valuable, son. Anything I can afford that makes my life just a tad bit easier."

Those words would spur us on our brainstorming session. We needed to think of something we could sell to those who really had the money. Something they needed. We had spent a few hours thinking with no result. We were taking a break when we heard the neighbors pull their car into their driveway. They had a classic Mercedes. I remembered looking down at it as the neighbors climbed out, imagining myself behind the wheel. Bryan joined me at the window, saw what I was looking at, and frowned.

"What?" I asked. "Isn't it a cool car?"

"The car is old school."

"Maybe I like old school."

"Yeah, yeah. I wouldn't touch the car with a six-inch pole," Bryan said as he climbed up the bunk beds, "even if it wasn't that dirty."

"What did you just say?"

"What?"

"Come on, you said something just now," I repeated, impatient.

"I said I don't want the car," Bryan said, annoyed.

"No, not that. Something about not touching it if it…"

"I wouldn't touch it with a six-inch pole, even if it wasn't that dirty."

"Bingo!"

Bryan looked confused and frustrated as I hurried around, looking for a pen. "What has gotten into you?"

"What if we helped people wash their cars?"

Bryan's mood changed immediately. "Not bad. Not bad."

"I know, right?" I exclaimed. It felt good to have finally hit on an idea. We had been thinking in terms of products we could sell to people, but we never thought about what we could do for people in exchange for money. We never thought about services.

"Hold up! Not just washing cars, we could do all kinds of things for people!" Bryan exclaimed.

"I know I know!" I yelped, too excited.

That night, Bryan and I decided we would go see our neighbors and ask if they would like us to wash their car for a small fee. Unfortunately, the following day when we returned from school, our neighbors had already had their cars washed. We were down for a short while, but then Bryan thought we should continue and try to sell off the rest of the candy we had at the house. As we approached our sixth house after three rejections and one house abandoned, we noticed the tall grass in front of the next house. Just then, Bryan whispered in my ear and my eyes lit up.

"Yes, we are going to offer that," I said.

We knocked on that door and asked whether they would buy candy and if not, whether they needed help with mowing their lawn. We got an instant yes.

That was how we began to trade in services.

Market First

Since the dawn of the industrial era, businesses have always had successes and failures, ebbs and flows. They are like microorganisms on this tiny cosmos of a planet, and like any organism, they are always vulnerable. They catch a fever, throw up, and declare their mortality or bankruptcy. According to the U.S. BLS (Bureau of Labor Statistics), about 45% of new businesses fail during their first five years, and that number reaches a whopping 65% during their first 10 years.

These statistics should not scare budding entrepreneurs. Instead, consider it an insight into the landscape of the business market. It is something to inspire you, challenge you, and give you a head start on what to expect and how to chart the course of your business. It's not an uncommon trend for start-ups to fail, and there are proven statistics to back up this claim. Research has it that nine out of every ten start-ups fail. In a 2015 Forbes publication titled 90% of Start-ups Fail: Here's What You Need to Know About The 10%, Forbes Contributor Neil Patel reviews the few areas that start-up entrepreneurs never overlook in the course of their venture. Bryan and I did our research and kept finding a major recurring issue that several entrepreneurs face. The number one reason why businesses fail is that the product they have developed is unsuitable for the market's demand.

What? How can people go out of their way to make a product, give their time and investment, and in the end, the market declares it unsuitable? How dare you?!

Before we go into a rage, let's take a closer look.

The truth is that several businesses are doomed to fail and you should know that it is nothing personal if it happens to you. The business market is a dog-eat-dog scenario where the most skilled and informed businesses do not necessarily make it to the top. Yes, that must seem deeply unfair, but luck also plays a role. You can be pretty good, come up with a great product that does X, Y, Z, and you can still fail if your product or service is not suitable to market demands or does not meet a specific need.

Whatever it is you are coming up with, be it an invention, a new kind of shaving powder or an app, it has to be such that people do not have to worry themselves about what its function is, how it could be used or how it would benefit their lives. Simply put, they don't have the extra time to learn. In the few seconds that you're trying to explain what value your product holds or how it works, they have already made up their minds about where to spend their money. And it's not with you.

The value of your product/service should be such that it can be easily spotted in an instant. Its design, its ease of use, its packaging; all these things are elusive factors that most entrepreneurs overlook. These are the aspects you must consider as you go about designing a product or service.

Of course, this might appear to be rather impossible in the creative industry. Everyone is an artist, you say, everyone is unique, or this doesn't apply to the creative industry because creativity is rewarded. As long as you put in all the hard work, there is no chance of your work bumming. Well, there's a pretty big chance if your work isn't entering an already existing market. Even if you're Steve Jobs, but even at that, there is a very slim chance of you experiencing success. Even Steve Jobs suffered a crisis.

The creative industry—entertainment: music, film, comics, books, etc.—is an industry propagated by fans, so these individuals may appear to be unaffected by this concept of a market need because there are already existing loyalists of specific creatives, whether authors, film directors or musical talents. However, the reality of the dilemma regarding market demand quickly creeps in when a creative entrepreneur starts to follow a trend and not trail-blaze, or do something entirely different, like coming up with a unique sound or a new narrative style or film technique. Following the bland process of just coming up with standard material quickly becomes something of a boring enterprise for both the creator and the consumer. Despite the hours of work that the creators have invested, the market quickly decides that the product has failed or is a failure.

Understanding the market in which one competes is too crucial to success. It's a hard smack in the face when a company sets out on a project that has no intrinsic market value. However, this only goes to say that the company had no eyes or ears on the market. They likely conducted no research and were more of a self-centered enterprise. This is a dangerous mistake to make in a world like ours, as brands without a solid PR team tend to take a big hit during such fails, if they survive at all. Before setting out or coming up with a product, a few questions entrepreneurs might ask are:

What are other brands/companies similar to our offering?

What kinds of complaints have been occurring in the market, and how are they being addressed?

How can we fashion our product/services to suit that niche?

While things like marketing and product placement are good tactics for making sales, because it is all about sales, too quickly a product that has no market value is revealed for the failure that it is. Quickly, all those sales you made only put your bad product in the hands of furious consumers who discover the poor quality of your product and bad mouth you and your brand out of business.

Yes, we have stressed just how vital it is to understand one's market. It is an invaluable skill that most entrepreneurs struggle to grasp. At the start of our music journey, Bryan and I were fans of artists like Tupac. His eloquence, energy, and the novelty to his lyrics, it was a package we found fascinating. More than our fascination with his word power, there was some intrinsic value to his words, a story we wanted to hear because we connected with it.

Tupac grew up in the ghetto, a rough, dog-eat-dog world where the constant battle with the authorities and other rival gangs was the only life he'd known. So when Tupac did rap, it wasn't a regular song from a regular person. It was a dynamic story, a live narrative of reality hitting the folks of the ghetto life right in the eye, and showing the rest of the world how bad it was. It wasn't just a 'nice, decorative product' kind of song. It was real, with real-life value, and although the genius of Tupac couldn't reach its peak before he died at 25, we can at least say that he truly was a pacesetter for the daunting path that every contemporary rapper had to come to terms with—the reality around us.

Our 'rags to riches' story isn't without its failures. Getting turned down by girls, nearly getting killed due to a bad purchase. There were nights, days, weeks and months when we doubted we could make it happen. We were hit with failure constantly. What helped?

We didn't cower and run away, no matter how bad it went. For one, something that kept us going was the support we received from folks we had met during our tour of California. Giving up was never on the table. We did come close, very much so. But we just couldn't. Remember, this is our life. Our life. We had nothing else to fall back on, and we weren't going to let anyone take it from us, so it had to work. It just had to. We were going to make it happen.

For every failure we have, Bryan and I, alongside our risk management pal, go over it together. Long before our risk control person was brought on board, when we were hit with some really serious issues, Bryan and I—who are usually aware of what has gone wrong—would discuss it together, consider what we did wrong, if we could have done it differently, and most importantly, how we could exploit and learn from the event to enrich our wisdom and ensure that our fans and customers still have an amazing experience.

It wasn't an easy task, and it still isn't. Long after having spent a few hours on stage, usually, there are meetings to attend, parties waiting, family responsibilities, etc. and having to sit through another meeting for damage control is the last meeting you want taking up your time. We think that, over the long haul, it's just as integral to the growth of any enterprise as advertising.

Know the Waters Well

One challenge that Bry and I faced before finally breaking into the limelight was that we didn't have much background knowledge about the music industry and how it functions. Remember, this was a time way before the internet boom, and we were just two brothers who caught a few lucky breaks. We were hungry for an audience, so we went for shows, featured at a few performances, but the gaps between those events were wide, and worse, the returns weren't worthwhile. We needed cash for gas and rent, so we took odd jobs along the way. It was certainly uncomfortable for two young minority boys seeking 'stardom,' as such work wasn't what we wanted to be caught doing. Yes, there is dignity in labor, but there wasn't a lot of respect for an artist who wowed an audience only to be caught working the day shift at a car wash or running the dishwasher at a diner. It wasn't what we found attractive. We wanted more of the glamour. We had to up our game plan.

Bryan and I started searching for sponsors. Instead of starting small, we sought out the big names in the industry. It was the trend. If you were an up and coming artist, you had to make contact with one of the big names. It was how you quickly revved up your visibility.

There was no Myspace, Facebook or Soundcloud where you could post your product for free and have it hit millions of streams. The only ways your song was played were radio houses, music TV stations, and the guys having a backyard party. It was pretty rough with no connections. We toiled to no end, trying to get our tape on the tables of the big names, but they were either too busy or we just didn't quite fit their mark.

I vividly recall an experience when Bryan and I were embarrassed during our search for industry connections. We had visited one of the big names in the music business at the time, we'll call him Big Nick. We received an invitation to Big Nick's space, a mansion sitting on some of the best land in California, overlooking a waterfall. Bryan and I walked in, having no idea we were about to experience the most embarrassing event of our lives.

We were told Big Nick would be with us shortly. A few minutes became a couple of hours. We waited for over four hours with still no word from Big Nick, and there was also no sight of the lady who had welcomed us at the door. When the lady had finally returned, Bryan spoke up.

"It's been a while now, could you tell him we're here—"

"Please be patient, Big Nick will be with you shortly."

I cut in. "That was the same thing you said about four hours ago—"

"Ryan," Bryan said, trying to calm me down. I sank back into the chair, staring daggers at the lady as Bryan turned to her.

"Please, we understand he might be busy. We've come a long way. Would you be kind enough to remind him that we're still here?"

"Big Nick will be with you shortly," she said, flashing a stoic smile as she walked off. Bryan cursed as he sank into another chair. My bones ached from sitting for so long. Two hours more and there was no word from Big Nick. Being upset doesn't describe it, because we were thinking of all the tasks we would have rather been getting done that would have generated some sort of value. The thought made us fume. Bryan kept assuring me that it would be over soon. Eventually, though, it was me telling him the same thing, that we'd invested too much time to just walk away. Finally, the door swung open and a fat man strode into the room, his voice gruff as he called on the lady who had walked us in. She wasn't nearby.

Bryan rose to his feet, as did I. The man looked in our direction, his eyes sharp and menacing. The man staring back at us was Big Nick.

"Who are you?" he said.

Bryan and I opened our mouths to talk, but I spoke first.

"We're the New Money Twinz. We've been waiting for you for the past six hours—"

"Get out of here," he said, but I'll spare you the language he actually used.

In a flash, a few security guards hurried into the room. They escorted us out of the mansion with our hands held behind our backs, their guns visible. I remember praying under my breath when I saw the weapons on these guys. We had heard of black people getting shot in the streets, their bodies left on the road to rot. I feared we would end up like that.

As they led us out, Bryan asked them be gentle with me, and I remember feeling my heart grind to a halt when a bulky guy with a tattoo of a flame on his neck glared at Bryan in response. For a moment, I watched him grip his gun tighter, and I could feel my heart and lungs tighten in my chest. He strode towards Bryan, raising the gun slightly, but the gates opened and a fleet of vehicles drove in. The bulky guy lowered the gun and we kept walking to the gate. Minutes later, they shoved us into the street and we ran for our lives. Literally.

That would be only our first experience with gatekeepers.

We had never heard anything about gatekeepers prior to that day. All we knew was that Big Nick was in the big leagues of the industry. We knew he had good connections; connections that could land us a real deal. We weren't sure how it all worked, but we wanted in. Unfortunately, we were more than a long shot from any sort of big break.

Now, according to Wikipedia, a gatekeeper is a person who controls access to something, for example, a city gate or bouncer that controls who is permitted entry or access to a category or status. Gatekeepers assess who is 'in' or 'out,' in the classic words of management scholar, Kurt Lewin.

Bryan and I would struggle with gatekeepers and what they represented. We simply couldn't get someone to slap their 'thumbs up' on our music, which was all we needed. It was difficult to perform at shows and hook up with a few guys who looked like they could help, only to be ignored immediately after. Initially, we thought they were just being snobs, intentionally ignoring us for one reason or another. Soon we would find out that they were legitimately busy people. They had lots of artists all over the world fighting for their attention, all of whom would send in their albums. And these albums piled up at a desk, most of which were never looked at once before hitting the trash bin. It's a wild part of the music world.

When Bryan and I caught on to how it worked, we knew it would be quite a while before we could reach out to the big guys. We'd wanted to break into the music business a little too quickly, not knowing the best path forward. We were young and ready, but we needed the right connections. We thought we needed some Big Nick to help us make it to the top. However, it turned out that all we needed were the few folks we had already met.

Right after the ordeal with Big Nick, we headed back to our benefactors, the couple with whom we stayed in California, the Damians. We would spend another series of months living on their couch, doing odd jobs while we rehearsed for shows in our spare time. The conversation that would alter our life happened in the third month of this pattern. I was in the kitchen reading an old book while Bryan walked quietly into the living room. Mrs. Damian was there, watching the news while she knitted in her sofa chair. I was snacking on an old-time favorite book of mine, Sherlock Holmes by

Arthur Conan Doyle, and I wasn't about to lose my pacing by checking on who had walked in. Here's a breakdown of what happened, according to Bryan.

So, I had walked home that evening, too exhausted to want to talk to anyone. I was calm when I got in, nodding curtly to Mrs. Damian, who smiled from the couch, still knitting those weird socks, but I could never call them weird to her face. She was too nice, although, I suspected she knew I thought the socks were weird as I had declined her offer to make some for me.

"You don't like the design?" she said in her slightly French Canadian accent.

"Umm, yeah—no. No, it's cool. Just not my thing," I said.

I walked past her, pulling off my sweatshirt so that my oversized grey tee was now visible, its armpit and chest regions damp from sweat. I walked into the garage, looking for something. I toiled for four to five minutes before I heard Mrs. Damian's voice creaking over the sound of the news broadcast coming to an end.

"What are you looking for?"

"One sec." I raised a hand, still pacing around, my head spinning for no reason. Ryan was in the kitchen curled behind that stupid book. I wanted to yell at him to dump that book and come help, but that wasn't how we operated. Mum never raised us to disrespect each other, emotions or not. Although, it was quite tempting, especially after the ordeal I had gone through that day.

I was ill the day before. But before falling ill, we had planned to visit the radio station and see the manager. We wanted them to play our song, no matter how unlikely. Of course, we didn't have the right amount of cash to pay for airtime, but we thought, 'what could possibly go wrong?'

And lo, Ryan, who had masterminded the idea himself, had also fallen ill. We didn't want the idea to die, though. We felt behind, as if time was running out, and we knew there had to be something we could be doing to push our brand. Ryan decided I could go on my own instead of wait for both of us to be well. So, I did. And I think I made a terrible deal.

"You did what?!" I remember hearing Mrs. Damian say after I finally sat down and told her what happened. From the corner of my eye, I saw Ryan stroll out of the kitchen, the book still in his hand, staring as if he was seeing me for the first time.

"What happened?" Ryan said, Mrs. Damian still staring like I had called her a rude name.

"What are you going to do now?"

"I don't know," I said, shaking my head. "I have no clue."

"What happened?" Ryan walked in, waiting for a response from either of us.

"I think your brother almost got you both in trouble," Mrs. Damian said as she recounted the story to Ryan.

That morning, I had left with Mr. Damian in his old Ford. He dropped me off at an intersection downtown, then I walked twenty minutes before reaching the radio station Ryan and I wanted to air our song. The security guy, a slim looking man with eyes that could penetrate the soul, asked what I wanted as he sized me up. For a moment, I watched a sympathetic frown form on his face.

"Here to see the manager," I said.

"Do you have an appointment?" he said.

I shook my head. "No, but I have a proposal that I think he will want to hear."

The guy stared at me, disbelieving, that sympathetic look still glued to his face.

"What could a guy like you possibly have for Mr. Switch?" he said. (I have changed the manager's name here for anonymity.)

"I understand you're doing your job," I said, taking a step closer, my eyes on the green nametag attached above his breast pocket, "but this may be the one deal that also changes your life, Mr. Oreon."

Five minutes later, I was ushered into the cozy, well-lit reception area by another guard. I was amazed by how fresh the place looked. There were posters on the walls, photos of artists, famous lines from their songs displayed next to them in stylish fonts. I smiled, dreaming about great it would be to have my face there someday, with my name, and my brother, of course. What line of ours would make it on the wall? It was that thought on my mind when a short, stout man walked in.

"You're the guy who's here to see me?" the man said, his voice surprisingly high-pitched.

"Are you the manager of the station?" I asked.

"No," the man said quickly, "I'm his boss."

I stood there, transfixed, trying to load more words worth speaking. I had thought I was ready for what was about to happen, but apparently I wasn't. Nowhere near ready. The thought of speaking to the owner of the radio house shattered my confidence instantly. I didn't register when the man asked me to follow him.

All I noticed was that he was walking away, and then he turned and tilted his head questioningly.

"Is everything okay?" he asked, confused.

"Uh, yes?"

"Then come along."

He led me into his office. I watched him recline in his high-backed seat as he offered me a chair. I declined.

"So, what deal do you have for me?" he said, his fingers loosely locked in his lap. I watched the balding part of his head, how shiny it was when light from the beautiful fixtures on the ceiling bounced off of it. Goodness, the silly details I spot when I'm nervous.

"I have a song, and I thought your radio house would want the opportunity to listen to it first," I said, trying to restore confidence.

"Well, we have procedures for things like this—"

"You do not understand," I said, leaning towards the table, my hands propped on it with sweat gathering under my armpits. "I can't afford the airtime money."

The man looked me in the eye and for a moment, I wanted to cower. I couldn't. I remember Dad telling me not to stutter, not to blink, or else I would lose. With every bit of muscle in my body, I maintained an unrelenting pose. My eyes hurt from not blinking, and I could feel strains as the tears started to boil up.

The man broke into a laugh. I didn't move.

"Oh, you're serious," he said.

I nodded.

"Well, we don't run a charity," he said, "and if you have any manners, you wouldn't walk in here and make ridiculous demands."

"I know how this may come off, but this deal means a lot to us," I said.

"Tell that to the guys at accounting, or to the tech guys who work hard to make this station run. See if their families can eat any meals on those words."

"Sir, I..."

"Enough, please leave my office," he said, already turning to paperwork.

I strode towards the door and turned.

"Just in case you change your mind," I said, pulling out a CD inscribed with The New Money Twinz and an address, then dropped it on his desk.

"See you around," I said, slamming the door shut behind me.

That was the only copy of the song Ryan and I had recorded. The only copy.

"What?!" Ryan yelled when Mrs. Damian was done narrating. For a moment, I feared he would pounce on me. "That was our only CD!"

"There was no other way."

"Couldn't you have just left and come back with it?" Ryan said through clenched teeth. I remained on the couch, throwing my head back to the cushion as I ran my hands through my hair. It was the only comfort I could find in the moment.

"How likely are they to get back to you?" Mrs. Damian said, trying to restore calm.

"I'm optimistic."

"How likely, Bryan?"

I licked my lips and sat up. "I don't know."

She let out a sigh as Ryan stormed off. I remember wondering where he had gotten all that energy from. Wasn't he supposed to be too ill to make the meeting?

"I don't know what to do, Mrs. Damian," I said, watching the fabric she was knitting absent-mindedly. "I don't even know if I want to do this anymore."

"Of course you do," she smiled. "You're only taking a few blows. It'll be worth it in a few months."

I scoffed. "Months. The sound of that scares me. It's been months for a while now."

"It shouldn't. The good things in life, the things that are worth it, tend to take time."

I sighed, annoyed at the truth in those words. I hated it when she made profound statements like that.

"What's on your mind now?" she said, still knitting.

"Nothing. Just here, wondering just how long we'll have to keep toiling in place, looking for someone who will help us, give us a break."

"Help you?" She stopped knitting. Her eyebrows seemed to rise as she spoke, as if I had just insulted her husband.

"Yeah," I said, watching her set the knitting wool down, fearing what would come next.

"You've got this all wrong, Bryan, if you're going into anything with the mindset that people will help you."

I sat there and thought. Here I was, with my brother, both of us in our early twenties, trying to get our names out there, and here she comes, acting as if we hadn't already given it all we had. I sat up and leaned forward.

"It would be good if Ryan were here while we talk about this," she said as she rose, calling my brother back to the room.

All three of us were seated at the dining table, with Ryan seated next to Mrs. Damian while I sat opposite them like some accused individual before a jury. Mrs. Damian had a flare for wisdom, but never had I been so humbled and inspired by her words.

"Going into any business or deal with the mindset that you need help is a good way to get yourself shot in the foot. Stop it. That is no way to earn respect. You both make great music, and you spend a lot of time at it. You can't be a lion at cooking good songs and be a chicken while getting your songs out there. You've got to earn your place."

Ryan looked confused, probably wondering what had led to the talk. I would explain later on, but at the moment, I was attempting to process Mrs. Damian's words.

"Are you saying we should stop trying to push our songs out?" Ryan said.

"No, absolutely not. I'm saying you've got to earn your place. And you don't do that by asking, or by getting a handout. You do that by being of value."

I scratched my head.

"How can we be of value to the big guys, the managers at the top? They don't need anything from us."

"Yes, they may look like they call the shots, but look closer. There are other means of getting your songs out. You know organizers, right? You know DJs, club managers. These are the folks you need to develop relationships with. They play others' music for a living. Offer them something of value and in return, you get to enjoy the leverage they command."

Mrs. Damian had made some solid points, I had to admit. Although I was wondering what service we would offer those folks that would be of value. Good thing I had a twin, because he had it figured out.

Gatekeepers Everywhere

Envy. Humans tend to hone in on things we do not have. We immediately recognize our weaknesses in the strengths of others. We say we don't have this and that, never taking time to acknowledge the few things we do have. It's the same with the current COVID crisis. Social interactions used to be just one of the many conveniences we all had on the course of making ends meet or achieving whatever agenda requiring interaction with other humans. The pandemic shifted all of that interaction. Some went virtual while others, who were sent sprawling into the abyss, flickered out of existence like a blown-out candle. You can tell that humanity misses social interactions, and proof of this is the number of people who keep marching out of their homes in the middle of supposed lockdowns, but, of course, this is not a passage on COVID. We're talking about entrepreneurial success during a time like this.

Just as the entire world immediately failed to value social interaction and is gradually coming to realize our deep need for it, so also had Bryan and I failed to see the gatekeepers around us, and the powers they held. It turned out that we already had the right set of folks necessary to push our songs out to the world. And they had just been there, waiting for us to tap into their potential.

After that conversation with Mrs. Damian, Bryan and I went to a popular club in the area, dressed for the occasion. While others were there smoking, talking, or doing whatever, Bry and I just sat there, observing the room. There was a DJ who was running the show and soon, Bryan was to head over to his side of the club and start a conversation, make a connection. That was his goal for the night, to win the club's DJ over to our side.

While Bry headed right for the DJ, I was seated, bored, pondering what I could do to help. I started a conversation with the bartender and soon we were talking about the store. In a matter of minutes, I knew about the bartender, and the business, and I felt assured we would make good progress that night. Well, I thought too soon, because we didn't get all the information we needed. We had to keep visiting the club, continuing conversations with the bartender and the DJ, building relationships.

Over the week, we established ourselves as good customers and great company, and finally, we were invited to make song selections. I was more than elated when Bry told me that the DJ had asked if we had any songs to add to the set list. They had always discussed which songs would set the mood for the night, and finally, he thought it would be the time to try one of our songs. Not to toot our horns or anything, but it was amazing. Truly amazing.

Bryan and I had managed to make another copy of the CD. Although Bryan had insisted it was no use, I figured we really needed to print it out, just in case. His idea was that the radio house might someday play our song, which would solve the problem. I didn't want to wait for someday, as our chances of ever getting a shot at the spotlight was slim, and slimmer every day they didn't play the song.

I remember spotting Bryan sitting by the radio day and night, hoping that our song would get played by Mr. Switch's radio house. Sadly, that day never came. Maybe they played it at some later time, we have no idea. And the truth is that we don't care. We were finally getting the exposure we wanted, earning it on our own. The club was a start. There was still a long way to go, but we were ready for the long haul.

The Big Leagues Want In

After we started making some serious waves in the club scene, we attracted a few sponsors. These were pretty major names who had sponsored superstars we looked up to. They approached us, saying they wanted to represent us. We made it! But Bryan wasn't thinking like that. Instead, he was worried.

"What's up with you, Bry? This is what we've worked so hard for. Why the moody look?" I asked minutes after we left the studio with another offer. Bry and I had hopped into the back seat of the studio's company car and were now being driven to a motel in the area. We had moved away from Mr. and Mrs. Damian about two years back.

"I don't know, man," he said. "This whole thing just feels uncomfortable. Something isn't right."

I knew what he meant. For the past two years, we had been running the show all by ourselves. We didn't get help from anyone, and we'd stopped looking for help. We had worked hard, trading favors with people who could put us on a few small stages, and soon, word had gotten out. The New Money Twinz was gradually becoming a name that made waves.

During that time, we had also printed some dollar bills with our name on them. Not legal tender, but it did have its purpose. It was a symbol, something that earned those who had it some degree of respect. Call it a symbol of a brotherhood, of sorts. Perhaps these thoughts were bothering Bryan.

"Want to take a while to think about it?" I asked as we pulled up to the motel.

"I guess so," Bryan said as we went to our room.

We would spend a long time trying to decide. The executives from the studio had sent in the contractual documents early on in the process. Thanks to Bry's uneasiness, we initially held back on signing the deal. We brought in a friend who happened to be a lawyer, as we couldn't afford to pay anyone else. It was one of the few times we'd accepted help.

I kept pondering why on Earth Bryan thought we needed one. I had heard of music artists getting ripped off by studios and record labels in the past, but it never occurred to me that the same could happen to us. Well, it could, and almost did, as our attorney pal explained. The contract turned out to be way less than fair. The benefits were terrible and what I had thought was a pretty sweet deal turned out to be a great deal of liability long after the tax money had been cut from the check. Factoring in the total amount of time we would dedicate to working for the label and the returns we would receive, our attorney friend shook his head.

"Bad deal," he said. "This is a set of golden handcuffs, boys. Lose it."

"Isn't there a way we could re-negotiate?" I said, thirsting not to lose the deal over some 'petty issues' that could be straightened up. Our lawyer shook his head.

"Listen Ry, I know this looks like a sweet deal. It isn't. It may work well for a few years, but in the long run you will suffer for it."

And so, Bryan and I let go of that deal, even though it hurt to do so. Today, though, I'm grateful for that pain.

For most young creatives out there, you must consider the long term. Learn to ask questions of unbiased and uncompromised professionals. If you are offered a contract, don't be swept by the whopping sums and the bubbling emotions. Trust me, all those figures you are seeing are rounded up to entice you. They will be taxed off and you will probably be left with spare change, an amount way less than what you would earn had you been working on your own, or with a company not out to steal from you.

Don't get us wrong, not all deals are like this. And hey, if you feel that working with a record label is the sure way to climb the ladder of success, why not? Go for it. Just be wary. Again, ask questions of qualified, unbiased professionals. By unbiased, we mean individuals who have nothing to gain or lose should you decided to accept or decline a contract. They have no money in the game.

BRYAN WOOD ON WHO IS AN ENTREPRENEUR, REALLY?

This was one question I never thought I would have a hard time considering. I used to think entrepreneurs were bums who were stupid enough to start businesses. In those days, to be called an entrepreneur made me cringe, similar to a salesman. Everyone wanted to work at the big corporations with the fancy offices. People were swarming to college to collect degrees so they could work at jobs that would secure them for life, allowing them a retirement filled with vacations and sports cars. That was the dream, anyway: go to school, get a job at some big corporation, outwork everybody else, save and then retire when you've served your time.

The stigma around entrepreneurs was such that you'd quickly change course if you weren't a strong, independent-minded individual. For us, though, we never cared about what people thought of us. We shed that feeling way back in middle school. We had gradually started securing more jobs, thanks to our twin-dependent efforts. There was always something to be done; searching for big events, figuring out who their event host/organizer was, planning the setup and set list, deciding on the amount of the cut we would take, things like that. It was stressful at first, but knowing we couldn't afford to hire a manager at the time was enough to push us. We accepted it as part of what we needed to do. We multi-tasked consistently and when we hit the bed, it was like we had hit the reset button, except that ours wasn't going to reset until about 6 AM the next day. We were budding entrepreneurs, the things we had once despised, and we had no idea.

Who is an Entrepreneur?

One of our favorite definitions of the term is derived from Crash Course Business: Entrepreneurs pop up in all types of industries and can have widely different backgrounds. Some build personal brands while others work tirelessly on a physical product that they believe in…at its core, an entrepreneur is someone who sees a need and takes on the financial risk of starting a business to fill that need.

Did we say being an entrepreneur was easy? Well, hopefully you know better. Entrepreneurship goes beyond just having some brilliant idea about a product or service. You have to be willing to take the financial risk that will ensure the feasibility of your project. It's so much more than having an idea. You have to be willing to put in the cash and show others how much you value that idea. For us, when we had gradually started making some money, we sent our songs to radio houses alongside the required stipend to ensure that our songs were aired. If you asked us at the time, the whole idea just seemed silly and a waste of our cash. But, our song was our product, right? And the radio houses appeared to be the vehicles that would help circulate our song, for a price. It wasn't a particularly amazing process at first. We recall having to work so hard for that money. Having to part with it so quickly was difficult, but we did it anyway and viewed it as an investment.

COVID AND ENTREPRENEURS

Now, in light of the COVID crisis, you may be wondering whether now would be a safe time to start a business. Well, it's the wrong way to look at it. The truth is if you're looking for a safe time to launch your idea, you'll be waiting a long, long time. There is no safe time in the world of business. We had intended this book to address folks who wanted to start a business after the pandemic, but there's no telling how long this will last. So, whether now a good time to start a business is the wrong question. Instead, ask what you need to do to start your business now.

At this point, lots of folks are staying at home, going about their various duties from the comfort of their bed or couch. For some, they spend longer periods at home with their family, something that could only have been a dream prior to the pandemic. Now, ask yourself the following: what products and services would I need if I were spending more time with my family?

Just to give you an idea, let's do a breakdown of what the average Joneses do every day. They wake, maybe brew their coffee while they prepare for the day. Mrs. Jones is most likely helping five-year-old Nora in her bathroom while Daddy showers in his. Ten minutes in, everyone is at the dining table, rushing their breakfast in time to beat the early morning traffic jams. While Mummy is feeding Nora, Nora spills cereal all over Daddy's suit jacket, which had been hanging on the seat next to hers. Daddy is upset as he hurries to grab his other suit, frantically checking his watch as he goes. The city bus will arrive in three minutes, so Daddy dashes to work.

Mummy takes Nora to the daycare and then heads over to her small grocery store downtown, where she has a few workers tending the small establishment. By two, she hurries to the daycare to pick Nora up. While she walks Nora back to the store, she spots a sundress she loves. She buys the product alongside a dress for little Nora, and a flashy tie for her husband. She heads back to the store, balances the books while one of her workers plays with Nora to keep her busy. Then, Mrs. Jones heads home to prepare dinner while Nora naps on a comfortable, movable bed designed to keep the outside noise filtered out. Mr. Jones arrives and after dinner, the two exchange kisses and hugs while Nora takes a second nap. Mr. and Mrs. Jones watch an old movie while each of them shares details from their day.

Having read all the above, re-imagine what it would look like if this couple never left home due to COVID. What would they need to carry out their daily tasks without any issues from not being able to step out? The answers you come up with are indicators of what people need during this pandemic.

For most of human history, periods of great uncertainty have always been filled with opportunities. It's like taking advantage of a storm by building a windmill. It's okay to have dreams, but the truth is that your dreams only mean something if you will commit to the work, to determine the intrinsic, long-term value your idea will bring. No matter what your dream is, if it doesn't add value or fill a specific kind of need of others, then you might need to abandon that dream and get another one. It may sound harsh, there are no two ways about it.

Dreams thrive when they are molded and worked into something that touches lives, whether it is you trying to figure out the cure to cancer, coming up with an algorithm that helps people navigate the hassles of deciding what products to use or where one can get the best coffee in town. It's all about people. It's all about touching lives and making a positive difference.

GEARING UP FOR A POST-PANDEMIC: Business Ideas for This Season

Here, we take on a very dry, matter-of-fact approach to starting a business during and after the pandemic. We will take a bit of a deep dive into seemingly-technical fields. You should know that these are topics we did not thoroughly research. We do not claim to be experts, so it would probably be wise to check with specific authorities/experts before embarking.

The Dawn of a Pandemic

December 31st, 2019, SARS-CoV-2, also known as COVID-19, was first reported in Wuhan, China and it has changed the world as we know it. No one expected a pandemic as we prepared for the beginning of a new decade. The pandemic ravaged economies around the world and thousands of businesses were brought to their knees. Millions of people lost their jobs, and the entire planet was on lockdown at one point or another. Despite several efforts by the governments of some countries to ease the burden inflicted on their people by the pandemic, millions still have overdue bills and loans to sort out. The silver lining in the cloud this tiny virus caused is that several vaccines have been developed in record time to combat this disease, and all we are waiting for is mass production and distribution. As we gradually move to the post-pandemic phase, the world's economies are trying to pick up the pieces of the destruction and restore stability to those who lost it. This book is to serve as a guide to establishing different businesses in the aftermath of this pandemic.

Even though several businesses were ruined, the pandemic made new millionaires and new businesses as these individuals were positioned to leverage the lockdown by providing services and technologies that made working from home easier. The internet has enabled several avenues that we can harness to make money. Several models of extracting money from the internet have been devised over the last two decades, and we will be looking at some of them now as we move towards the end of the pandemic. Some of the ideas discussed here are capital intensive, while others involve the rendering of services to others. These skills can be learned on different free and premium platforms on the internet such as YouTube, Udemy, Coursera, etc.

VIRTUAL BUSINESSES

This pandemic has shoved us forward in time. By that, I mean that we are beginning to adopt some business models that otherwise would have come into use some ten years from now. Different ways of learning, buying, selling, etc. which were not popular have rapidly become the norm. Words like drop shipping and virtual learning have entered the modern lexicon. In this section, you'll learn how to sell various skills and services online.

DROP-SHIPPING

This is a business model that involves a retailer selling goods to consumers without coming into contact with the goods. Instead, the goods are shipped from the manufacturer or wholesaler directly to the customer. This business model has been popular for some time and it can be capital intensive depending on several factors, such as the location of your clients and how difficult it is to ship the products you sell.

You can be a physical or virtual retailer depending on whatever works best for your situation. A physical retailer has an actual store where he or she keeps the goods he or she intends to sell and (not required but necessary) a website to display the goods he or she has in the store. A virtual retailer only has a website where he or she displays the goods for sale. In this case, the goods are shipped directly from the producer or the wholesaler to the consumer, although it is possible to customize the goods before they are shipped to the consumer. You can come up with whatever arrangement suits you and your supplier on that.

Things to consider before starting up a drop-shipping business

1. Sell something that you are passionate about, because you need the extra motivation that will propel you to keep at it when things get tough. A lack of interest will make you quit before you even find your footing, especially when you are disconnected from the physical product.
2. Carry out intensive research on your competition. Unless your research says otherwise, try not to venture into selling products with low competition as they tend to have low demand, making such a potential model unfeasible. Research is vital, as it provides insight into problems that are present in your chosen niche and how you can leverage them to make massive sales.
3. Select goods that are easy to ship. Doing this will help eliminate high shipping fees for your customers, making the goods relatively affordable. Selecting something cheap also allows you to give your customers the option of free shipping without damaging your bottom line. This also provides you the opportunity to shave off some profit comfortably and occasionally offer a discount for your customers. These small tips are very important as they will attract a lot of customers.

4. It is very important that whatever you are selling appeals to potential customers that can afford to buy without thinking twice. This can be done by selling uncommon products that are still useful in our day-to-day activities. Also, ensure people can easily search for and find whatever you are selling.

5. Getting a quality supplier is crucial with dropshipping. A good supplier will make sure you have goods reliably supplied to your customers with neck-breaking speed. Quick delivery will lead to more customers. Communication and trust are very important between you and your supplier, as it facilitates smooth and efficient business transactions. Some of your suppliers can be in different countries, so communication is critical to keep the products moving.

6. In designing your website, make sure it is readily visible to potential customers upon entering key words in their search bar. This can be achieved by search engine optimization. To achieve good search engine optimization, you need to be versatile and knowledgeable with the keywords in your niche. Also, upload useful content on your site regularly as this increases visibility when people input certain words in their search engine.

7. Harness the power of social media ads in attracting potential customers. Taking advantage of the ads available on social media apps like Facebook, Twitter, and Instagram is very important in attracting potential customers as social media has become a huge part of millions of lives. Also, having a very interactive social media account is advised. You can organically gain followers and ultimately potential customers through these accounts via giveaways, subscribing for shout-outs, and subscribing for ads on the accounts of social media influencers.

8. One of the ways to earn your customer's trust is to make sure that the product you deliver matches the one on your website. Before you start your drop-shipping business, you must order a sample of your desired merchandise to ensure its authenticity and quality. This will prevent your customers from getting substandard products, which will ultimately affect your ratings. Make sure the quality is worth the cost.

9. Try to work with several suppliers, because relying on a single supplier might cause delivery delays. A single supplier might run out of stock, or suffer any other issues that can negatively affect a business. We all know that speedy delivery is crucial.

10. Make sure you target customers from all over the world. This is an advantage of drop shipping; the ability for you to deliver goods anywhere without worrying about shipping or delivery fees and customs duties.
11. When you start drop-shipping, do not invest tons of money into it. Instead, try to test the market and see if your customers will love your products. It is advisable for you not to order anything until a customer orders something, to conserve money.
12. Diversify your offerings. This will not only increase your income but will help you with an alternative if one store stops producing income. Also, make sure you track your goods as they leave your supplier to your consumer to prevent cases of missing goods and subsequent breach of trust.

ADVANTAGES AND DISADVANTAGES OF DROP-SHIPPING

Before you dive into drop-shipping, it is very important to know some of the advantages and disadvantages of operating a store operates under this system.

ADVANTAGES OF DROP-SHIPPING

- Low start-up cost: Starting up a drop-shipping business is significantly cheaper than starting up a regular retail store. Drop-shipping eliminates the problem of renting or building a warehouse and/or a shop and filling it with goods, cost of the store inventory, and manpower. Drop-shipping requires money for setting up your online store or for renting a space on drop-shipping sites like Shopify, and money for social media ads. The cost of running ads on social media is relatively affordable, making drop-shipping cost-effective in almost all aspects.
- The ability to offer products instantly: Unlike regular retail stores in which the store owner has to wait until she has goods in stock before offering them, a person running an online drop-shipping store doesn't have to wait for anything before displaying or offering whatever product she intends to sell. Instead, she simply puts her products online, and when a consumer chooses to buy, the owner of the store simply reaches out to his or her supplier, who sends it to the customer.
- Offering and testing varieties of products without risks: Drop-shipping gives one the advantage of offering a wide range of products without the need for worrying about the cost of

purchase and storage space. One can have various goods on display on her website, unlike conventional retailers who have to worry about logistics and costs. Also, drop-shipping allows one to test how new products will perform in the market without having to risk any amount of money in the process. Understanding what customers want can be hard work in conventional retail stores, but drop-shipping affords you the opportunity to easily get rid of products that do not sell.

- Not time consuming and laborious: Drop-shipping easily eliminates the time that conventional retail stores consume on things like packaging, branding, labeling, and shipping by allowing the owner of the store to easily contract them to third party organizations, which give the owner of the store more time for other areas of the business.

DISADVANTAGES OF DROPSHIPPING

- Getting a reliable supplier: This can prove problematic as most of the producers and wholesalers of the products you want to sell are in countries different from yours. Most people can easily get scammed if they don't secure someone trustworthy. Research is vital when it comes to drop-shipping suppliers.

- Entering a high-profit niche: This is also difficult, as the niche one is interested in might be overcrowded, therefore reducing one's chances of making a tangible profit. This, coupled with shipping fees and other expenses, can reduce the profit margin drastically if the niche high in competition.
- Lack of proper information: Before drop-shipping goods, it is important to have enough information about the product. Unfortunately, most people don't carry out adequate research before they begin to sell. This can become problematic as adequate information of whatever product you intend on selling has to be derived from testing or using the said product, often at the expense of the consumer. Not having enough information about what you sell can be disastrous for your business as your prospective customer might want to know as many things as possible before they buy it.

DROP SERVICING

Drop servicing, like drop-shipping, requires moving something from someone to another while making a profit, but unlike drop-shipping where goods are moved, services are moved. In drop servicing, someone connects a freelancer to a client for a fee, or, technically, you outsource whatever services you can't render for a client to someone who can. This has become a lucrative business as the world of freelancing is getting crowded and the fees one gets on freelancing sites like Upwork and Fiverr are relatively cheap. Unlike drop-shipping, where you earn profits per goods delivered, drop servicing has the hidden advantage of one's earnings depending on the contract between freelancer and the client. Some gigs may last for months, and the client often pays on a monthly basis. Also, you don't necessarily need a specific skill to enter. All you need to do is to collect high-paying clients who provide you a gig and you outsource it to a freelancer.

FREELANCING

Freelancing is referred to as a profession that involves a person (freelancer) using a specific set of acquired skills to render services to differing clients. This is referred to as a situation where you use your education (formal or informal) to render services to different individuals instead of sticking to a single employer. Freelancing often involves a freelancer receiving jobs (referred to as gigs) that can be fulfilled from home. This is different from the regular "working from home" jobs that became popular during the pandemic because working from home means you are still committed to an employer or an organization, unlike freelancing, where you work with different clients on different gigs of your choosing.

Unlike regular jobs, freelancing gives you complete flexibility with the work you decide to take. Jobs (gigs) can be short-term (a couple of days to a couple of weeks) or long-term (a couple of months to a year or a few years). One of the requirements of being a freelancer is having a skill or skills, as this is what you are selling to your clients. In this section of the book, we will talk about some of the high-earning skills, websites where you can get gigs, and the pros and cons of freelancing.

HIGH EARNING SKILLS

It is one thing to have skills that can attract gigs, and it is another thing for to have skills that are in high demand. Skills like copywriting, web development and design, data analysis, blog writers, etc. are in high demand in the freelancing industry. In this section, we shall examine some of them in detail.

WEB DEVELOPMENT

Web development is defined as the process of creating websites, web pages, virtual businesses, social network service providers, and web applications that run on the internet, or in a private network that is used in organizations (known as an intra network, or intranet). Web development doesn't deal with the design and aesthetics of a website; instead, it deals with all the code and programs vital to the smooth running of a website or web application. Web development may sometimes involve client-side scripting, server-side scripting, development of web content, creation of web servers, etc.

You may hear people use the words web development and web design interchangeably, but they are not the same thing. As stated earlier, web development deals with the coding and programming necessary for a website to run, but in the case of web design, it involves everything related to what the user sees, like user experience design (UX), user interface design (UI), etc.

Web development can be divided into three parts, namely; server-side coding is also known as back end, client-side coding also known as front-end, and database technology.

- Client-side scripting (front-end development): This aspect of web development is involved with the part of the website that the user sees. It simply refers to everything related to user experience and user interface. Front-end powers up the colors, fonts, and layouts of the site. Programming languages involved in front-end development include HTML, CSS, JavaScript, ECMA script, etc.

- Server-side scripting (back-end development): This aspect of web development is involved with building everything that runs in the background when you visit a website. Some of the things that happen in the back-end are acceptance of a user's data, like email addresses, names, phone numbers, etc., storage, organization and retrieval of that data, and making sure that everything on the front-end runs smoothly. Some programming languages used in back-end development/server-side scripting include java, python, ruby, etc.
- Database technology: The database is the part of the website that stores and helps with the retrieval of clients' data, along with assisting a website's dynamics.

Some websites do not run with a back-end. Such websites are known as static websites because there is no interaction between the user and the website. These kinds of websites are used for displaying information. Websites with both front-end and back-end are called dynamic websites or dynamic web applications because you can interact with them in ways like storage of data, modification of inputted data, and retrieval of information. The contents (front-end) of a dynamic website can change based on what is on the back end of the website.

In web development, one can decide to be a front-end developer, a back-end developer, or a full-stack developer. A front-end developer is concerned with engineering the front-end or the client-side of the website while a back-end developer engineers the back end of the website, or the server-side. A full-stack developer is a software engineer that manages both the client-side and server-side of a website.

COPYWRITING

This is the art of composing text with the aim of promoting and advertising goods and services. The crafted document is referred to as a 'sales copy' or 'copy.' Copywriters craft content that is found on billboards, brochures, social media posts, sales letters, commercials, and jingles, etc. Copywriters are employed in any agency and business whose aim is to make as many sales as possible, because advertising is vital to every business. They can also be employed by copywriting agencies whose sole aim is to help boost other businesses.

Let's examine some tips on how to be a good copywriter.

Tips on Being a Good Copywriter

As stated earlier, copywriting plays a critical role in advertisement campaigns. It is very important to exploit and magnify the strengths of whatever you are advertising. Every customer wants to know how a product will benefit them, and exploiting the strengths of the product will be of great advantage to your client. To be clear with the perks of the product, it is important to conduct an in-depth study of said product to discover its strengths and determine a way to magnify them.

Another important tip for writing good copy is to study your competition. This should be done to understand their weaknesses and exploit those in your sales copy or advertisement campaign by subtly showcasing them to your target audience, thereby demonstrating why patronizing the competition would be a poor decision. Exploit whatever the competition is offering that is inferior to what you are advertising. This will give your target audience motivation to patronize the product you are advertising.

Audience research is also important, as this will provide insight into the demographic you are targeting. This information will help you maximize the sales copy you have written by giving you more information on where to place the advertisement and what your customers understand. Try to understand your target audience and write what will appeal to them, specifically. A good understanding of the medium you intend on using to convey the information in your copy is a key to success, as every advertising medium has different styles and lengths of writing required to make it successful.

Try not to make the sales copy too wordy or technical. Humans have a short attention span, and once your sales copy doesn't appeal to them, it will be ignored and a potential customer will be lost. Try to make it as catchy as possible with words that will help capture and hold their attention.

Editing and proofreading one's work before publishing it on your desired medium is very important because if your sales copy has errors, it will create an impression of nonchalance on the part of your potential client, and it might discourage them from patronizing your client's business.

Other areas of freelancing include technical writing, software development, system analysis, accounting jobs, article writing, and so on.

Pros and Cons of Freelancing

Pros

- Freelancing gives one the ability to select their clients. This is crucial because working with someone whose temperament is similar to yours tends to increase your productivity as you both understand yourselves and can easily reach a compromise. Freelancing also gives one the opportunity to work with as many clients as possible, depending on one's choice. Freelancing gives one the ability to control the amount of work he or she wants to take on at a time, thanks to its flexibility and freedom.
- Freelancing provides independence, as you can work whenever you want without necessarily adhering to a strict schedule. This is also good for those who prefer to work independently and on their own schedule.
- The ability to work on several areas in your chosen niche as a freelancer cannot be overemphasized. Working for a company or an organization doesn't give this much freedom, as an organization would most likely allow one to specialize in a slim area in one's niche. The abil-

ity to work on as many things that interest you helps in broadening one's horizons and improving one's general knowledge.

- The earning potential of a freelancer is limited only by time and your success rate of attracting clients. As long as you have the ability to deliver, you get paid.

Cons

Depending on your country of residence, you might pay more in taxes as a freelancer than as a regular employee. In countries like the United States, taxes like the self-employment tax can be a huge factor in discouraging people from freelancing. Despite back doors in the laws guiding self-employed people that can be easily exploited by freelancers, most aren't aware of them, and unless you obtain a lawyer who can help you with the interpretation of the law, you'd most likely end up not using it to your advantage.

Unlike regular jobs that come with benefits such as sick leave, maternity leave, and medical insurance, being a freelancer doesn't come with perks like that. They literally have to sponsor their health insurance themselves.

Another issue with being self-employed is the fact that there is no steady pay, and freelancing being a form of self-employment is no different. One doesn't get a steady stream of clients, and this can affect cash flow significantly. Being a freelancer can be stressful because you have to treat your brand like a business (because it is a business), and running a business is just like caring for a child. You have to be concerned with things like branding, promotions, and the purchase of tools that are necessary for your chosen niche. While some software you will need is free, some are paid, and others have premium features that will be necessary to run your business smoothly.

Being a freelancer almost always requires one to be skilled in a certain area and for one to be able to carry out the tasks stipulated by the job. Thus, training and vast experience is always a requirement. Often, potential clients ask for previous jobs and certifications during interviews, and these can't be acquired overnight. They require months of training and practice for one to gain the substantial knowledge necessary to secure a gig.

AFFILIATE MARKETING

Affiliate marketing is a means of earning money by referring people to purchase a particular product or to use a certain service. Affiliate marketing predates the internet. In the past, people earned commissions by simply referring people to buy a product or use a service. The internet has made affiliate marketing easier as one can generate a huge amount of traffic (or audience) with a hyperlink. Some tips and tricks on how to do so will be discussed here.

Affiliate marketing is a very lucrative way of making money with little start-up capital. All you need is a large audience interested in what you are advertising and you are good to go. There are several ways to generate traffic that will help propel your affiliate marketing business. A popular method is to paste your referral link on your blog. Another is through email marketing. There are diverse methods for collecting the email addresses of potential customers. While some people randomly generate emails and use the ones that work, others get theirs by purchasing them from those who collect people's mailing addresses on the internet either legally or illegally. Some may advertise on social media with their special referral link similar to the case of drop-shipping, but unlike drop-shipping, affiliate marketers are not concerned with shipping fees, the burden of searching for suppliers (as they have come to a certain agreement with the supplier on how they will help get their products to a wider audience), and the rest. Also, affiliate marketers earn a percentage of the selling price of the product (between 8 to 10 percent), and unlike dropshipping, where the profit margin depends on several factors, nothing affects the amount of money affiliate marketers earn.

HOW AFFILIATE MARKETING WORKS

Most companies like Amazon depend on creatives such as bloggers and social media influencers to help get their product to a wider audience. Apart from harnessing the power of social media ads and blogs for promotion, some creatives use other means, like fusing the products into skits, hilarious Twitter threads and such, so when their followers see these, they also see the products being advertised. In most cases, they put their unique link in the description of their social media content, and the potential customer is sometimes given a discount for using the link to purchase the goods or services. To create a strong affiliate program, three parties are involved; the manufacturer (or seller) of the product, the affiliate marketer, and the customer.

The seller or the manufacturer of the said product or service is the base requirement in this relationship triangle as without him or her, the product or service does not exist. This is the person who gives the contract to the affiliate because he/she either doesn't have the technical know-how to reach a larger audience, or he/she wants it to get to an even larger audience.

The affiliate marketer or the creative is the one who designs the advertising campaign to convey the product to a larger audience. He or she does this by either creating content with the sole purpose to advertise the product, or directly advertising the said product or service to a target audience in content such as video tutorials that explain the product to the audience, especially if the content is related to the product.

The consumer is the most important member of this triangle as without him, no one will purchase the said product, and that is against the sole objective of the campaign (to sell something). In some cases, the creative discloses how much he or she will receive on every purchase, and there is almost always no increase in the selling price of the goods and services being displayed because the affiliate marketer and the seller share the profits from the sale. It doesn't matter if the consumer knows the technicalities behind the whole thing. The most important thing in affiliate marketing is to determine if what one is selling is reaching the consumer.

There are three major ways in which an affiliate marketer earns money, and they are based on three different criteria:
1. The number of people who purchase the goods,
2. The number of people who click on the link placed in the content that has been created, and
3. The number of people who visit the producer's or seller's website to either complete a purchase,

download a tool or file, or sign up for anything like newsletters.

AFFILIATE MARKETING CHANNELS

There are many channels that an affiliate marketer can utilize while promoting a product or service. The end goal is creativity. Some of the ways in which you as an affiliate marketer can reach out to your target audience include:

Vlogs or YouTube: Most products are affiliated via vlogs and YouTube channels, especially if the YouTube channel is related to the product. This happens mostly for digital products like online courses, e-books, etc. A very good example is that of a programmer who runs tutorials on YouTube and affiliates for software required to create the said program.

Social media: This is a strong avenue for one to affiliate for products and services, especially physical products. On different social media, there are influencers with large numbers of followers based on the content they post. Most of the time, they actually influence the lifestyles of their followers and due to this, they can convince many of their followers to subscribe to a product or a service successfully.

Blogs: Blogs are also a strong avenue for affiliating products and services. This is also an excellent way to monetize blogs with a huge number of readers, as one can just paste his affiliate link in the blog after designing an advert for it. Most blogs are not coded from scratch as there are other mediums in which one can create a blog or a static website without coding. In this case, the intending affiliate marketer just pastes his affiliate link on the "back-end" of his or her blog, and it displays as an ad.

E-mail lists or e-mail marketing: This is an outdated of affiliating products and services, but it is still quite effective. There are several ways in which one can obtain the email addresses of prospective customers. The best is via the newsletter. You tell people to subscribe to your newsletter, where you share exclusive content on how to carry out a task, or tips and tricks in a particular niche, and you insert your affiliate link into the newsletter and send it out to subscribers. Another effective way to conduct email marketing is by building an email list and sending emails containing whatever you want to promote.

ADVANTAGES OF AFFILIATE MARKETING

Most people engage in affiliate marketing for passive income. Unlike a regular job that involves working between eight to twelve hours, affiliate marketing doesn't involve such stress. Once the content has been created and uploaded, the affiliate marketer keeps earning money on the affiliated product even in their sleep, as long as the content being created for the product or service keeps generating sales.

The fact that affiliate marketers don't have to deal with customers directly is another reason why most people engage in it. This is especially beneficial for those who are excellent creatives but either lack the cash to hire a customer service representative, or lack good people skills, as it provides a way to earn from their content without having to interact with customers. And apart from answering a few questions on how the said product or service works (which happens rarely), or by organizing a contest or some other event to drive the sales campaign, most affiliate marketers don't make contact with the customers.

Affiliate marketing offers the opportunity to work from home, and this provides a huge amount of independence as you can work whenever you want without necessarily adhering to a strict schedule or dress code. This is also good for those who prefer to work independently and at the times they are most comfortable with.

The overall cost of setting up an affiliate marketing business is very low compared to other businesses. This is because it follows a simple formula, which is to get the products or services to as many people as possible. Once you can get a good number of potential followers through social media, blogs, vlogs, or podcasts, and you can create very good content, you are good to go.

DISADVANTAGES OF AFFILIATE MARKETING

The major problem with affiliate marketing is generating the required traffic to jump-start the whole process. Gathering traffic to help propel your affiliate marketing can be difficult, as it is not easy to build a following on social media, YouTube, and blogs and podcasts. Creating relatable and useful content might be difficult for most people; being creative requires a lot of mental power.

Some products that you wish to affiliate with are relatively cheap, so you need to have a huge amount of people buying them in order to make a substantial profit. This is the case with affiliating e-books, software, and other digital products. With piracy on the rise, most people will seek out alternatives to obtaining such downloadable resources rather than purchasing them.

Some products or services that you really like and can vouch for might not have an affiliate marketing program, and this will lead to one carrying out a huge amount of research in order to prevent one's reputation from being damaged (especially if you are making a review for the intended affiliated product or service for your YouTube channel, blog or podcast).

Sometimes, to craft a good review for your channel, you have to buy the product, and this might be expensive. This isn't the case for everyone running a review on a product, though. It is also possible to secure a sample of a product before running a review of it, especially if you have a reputation on your social media account.

VIRTUAL SERVICES

We all are aware that the pandemic has restricted our movement, and except for emergencies, it has been advised that people stay home as much as possible. Because of these precautions, several jobs have been "lost" and different activities that people do both out of necessity and for leisure have been placed on hold. This part of the book aims to help those who used to have regular jobs and then lost them and/or their clients due to the pandemic. People like fitness coaches, therapists, teachers, dieticians, etc. can utilize the opportunity to continue doing what they love to do, which was sidelined due to the pandemic. Creating an online presence can be difficult at first, but with a few tricks, you should be up and running quickly.

Rendering services online isn't something new, but it's rapidly becoming a requirement during the post-pandemic period. Services that can be rendered online include virtual fitness coaching, virtual therapy, teaching, coaching and mentoring, etc. All these can be conducted virtually. Take a virtual fitness coach, for example; he or she can design an application that would help his or her clients reach their fitness and health goals. Some people might not have the natural discipline to exercise without proper monitoring, so he or she can schedule virtual meetings on apps like Zoom, where he or she will be able to physically monitor the clients as they exercise. Alternatively, syncing a wearable device with the app can help monitor the person's fitness progress.

Teaching online is becoming vitally important during this period as physical learning has been on hold in several major cities due to the pandemic. Most students will be receiving their lectures online, and they would most likely need extra assistance to make up for the lack of personal interaction. You as a teacher can come up with a Facebook advert or any other social media advertisement (or contract it out to someone who is an expert at making one) that you feel will reach as many potential students of yours as possible, telling them how you can help them achieve strong grades by instructing them in ways that they would understand, since most of them are just getting used to this new way of receiving information. These classes can be held online, or you can conduct door-to-door lectures while strictly adhering to the health guidelines stipulated by healthcare professionals to help navigate the pandemic. Alternatively, you can design an entire course on a particular field of learning that would interest not only students, but those who wish to learn the skill taught, and place them on learning platforms like Udemy, Udacity, and so on where students who are interested in both learning and expanding their portfolio will pay for these courses and learn.

This opportunity is not only open to teachers. This is something for whoever has a skill that is worth learning. Skills ranging from coding to baking to design to the playing of musical instruments can be designed into courses and uploaded to these learning platforms, and people who are interested will purchase these courses to learn and receive valid certificates upon completion of the program. To help make the course more understandable, you can design quizzes and paste links to resources you feel will be useful for their learning of the course. The better your course, the more sales it will generate for you.

Now, this is for the computer experts among us. It's no news that the world is undergoing a revolution, and almost everything that would be conducted physically is now done virtually. In the previous sections of this book, the emphasis was on businesses and brands needing an online presence more than ever if they want to make sales. Since most people and businesses don't have much technical know-how, computer experts can monetize their knowledge by serving as consultants for companies and businesses.

As an IT consultant, you offer advice for everything technical related to the business. To increase your chances of being employed and to have a shot at being well paid, you'll want to earn some certification from a reputable source to prove you are an expert in the said field (which is information technology). You can work remotely if you are a consultant, even if you have to do some technical work like penetration testing, bug hunting, general cybersecurity inspections, development of databases, and so on. Irrespective of your niche, as a person who renders virtual services, advertisements are critical as they are the only means you have to reach potential clients.

As a computer expert, it is necessary to have a robust profile on platforms like GitHub, Stack Overflow, and LinkedIn. Most people searching for IT consultants go to their profiles on the aforementioned platforms, so it is very important you have an outstanding profile. Twitter is also a good place for you to find companies to work with as it is a tech-inclined social media platform. You can place these links on your social media profile with a useful tool called Linktree. You can also start up a tech support call center; a platform to receive calls and assist people with tech-related issues ranging from how to use an app or software to how to set up a web page and the like. People are still trying to adapt to using new tools for tasks like working remotely and learning, so you will be someone who helps address issues they come in contact with as they navigate their way through the said application or software.

LOGISTICS

In a post-pandemic world, the movement of provisions and other merchandise from one place to another is of great importance and can be easily monetized. The fact is that most goods are bought online, so they would need to be moved from a warehouse, general store, and so on to its final destination: the customer's door. As stated earlier, food items, drugs, and other essential items purchased online would need to be delivered, and you can easily set up a logistics system in your home to fill that need. Now, creating a small logistics network isn't that hard, especially if you have a personal means of transportation like a car or a bike. You can simply move the said items from your home (once they arrive) to the doorstep of the final consumer. If you have enough resources, you can acquire more vehicles to assist in moving the said products from their origin to the doorsteps of the final consumers. All you need to do is to liaise yourself with a store or company that sells essential items and helps ship them to their customer. While doing this, you should be aware that obeying the laws and guidelines set by healthcare professionals is mandatory not only to protect one's health (and the health of your clients) but to help protect the reputation of your logistics network and the company you're working with, as this is essential for the growth of your logistics network system.

It's a Wrap

Congratulations on making it to the end. It must have taken courage. There are thousands of resources out there that will help you on your journey towards starting a business and making headway in life. This book is merely a starting point. Remember, the path to financial breakthrough and fulfillment isn't straightforward. It's a journey, not a destination. We hope you find that one thing that makes your heart burn. Until we see you again, it's goodbye from the New Money Twinz.

Further Reading:

We figured you guys might want to do some further reading. Truth is, we read but not as often as we would like to. We perused the web for a while and eventually we found stacks of books that people find incredibly insightful. You should know though, most of the books highlighted here were dubbed from the website: mondovo.com.

See https://www.mondovo.com/books/must-read-business-books/ for the entire reading list.

Of course, you don't have to read every book on this list. It might be great to read through a few book summaries from time to time and see which one you think would greatly benefit you. Good luck and have a blast exploring this list.

**note: the ratings on each books express the opinion of Mondovo.com, not that of the New Money Twinz

1. The Leadership Campaign

by *Scott Miller*

This book is a playbook for winning in the reality of today's competitive global business environment. Each of the 10 steps it offers was learned on the most intensely competitive global battlefields.

Our Rating: 4.6/5

2. eSCAPE: The 4 Stages of Becoming A Successful Entrepreneur

by *Anik Singal*

Pure Entrepreneur Development. This book gives you the step by step formula and skills set required to become a successful Entrepreneur. Anik Singal explained his own journey and problems and tell his reader how he overcomes it.

Our Rating: 4.56/5

3. Thirst: A Story of Redemption, Compassion, and a Mission to Bring Clean Water to the World

by *Scott Harrison*

In Thirst, Harrison recounts the twists and turns that built charity: water into one of the most trusted and admired nonprofits in the world. Renowned for its 100% donation model, bold storytelling, imaginative branding, and radical commitment to transparency.

Our Rating: 4.55/5

4. Expert Secrets: The Underground Playbook for Creating a Mass Movement of People Who Will Pay for Your Advice

by *Russell Brunson*

This book is PACKED with valuable and actionable insights! Easy to read too. His discussion of how to craft a pitch is priceless. Understanding that people don't make decisions firstly intellectually, and how to give them a reason to want to investigate your product is great.

Our Rating: 4.49/5

5. Big Debt Crises

by *Ray Dalio*

For the 10th anniversary of the 2008 financial crisis, one of the world's most successful investors, Ray Dalio, shares his unique template for how debt crises work and principles for dealing with them well. This template allowed his firm, Bridgewater Associates, to anticipate events and navigate them well while others struggled badly.

Our Rating: 4.47/5

6. Bad Blood: Secrets and Lies in a Silicon Valley Startup

by *John Carreyrou*

The full inside story of the breathtaking rise and shocking collapse of Theranos, the multibillion-dollar biotech startup, by the prize-winning journalist who first broke the story and pursued it to the end, despite pressure from its charismatic CEO and threats by her lawyers.

Our Rating: 4.46/5

7. Shoe Dog: A Memoir by the Creator of Nike

by *Phil Knight*

In this candid and riveting memoir, for the first time ever, Nike founder and CEO Phil Knight shares the inside story of the company's early days as an intrepid start-up and its evolution into one of the world's most iconic, game-changing, and profitable brands.

Our Rating: 4.45/5

8. The Dichotomy of Leadership: Balancing the Challenges of Extreme Ownership to Lead and Win

by *Jocko Willink*

The Dichotomy of Leadership, Jocko and Leif dive even deeper into the uncharted and complex waters of a concept first introduced in Extreme Ownership: finding a balance between the opposing forces that pull every leader in different directions. Here, Willink and Babin get granular into the nuances that every successful leader must navigate.

Our Rating: 4.40/5

9. Leadership: In Turbulent Times

by *Doris Kearns Goodwin*

In Leadership, Goodwin draws upon the four presidents she has studied most closely—Abraham Lincoln, Theodore Roosevelt, Franklin D. Roosevelt, and Lyndon B. Johnson (in civil rights)—to show how they recognized leadership qualities within themselves and were recognized as leaders by others. By looking back to their first entries into public life, we encounter them at a time when their paths were filled with confusion, fear, and hope.

Our Rating: 4.40/5

10. Never Split the Difference

by *Chris Voss*

A former international hostage negotiator for the FBI offers a new, field-tested approach to high-stakes negotiations—whether in the boardroom or at home.

Our Rating: 4.39/5

11. The Laws of Human Nature

by *Robert Greene*

Robert Greene is a master guide for millions of readers, distilling ancient wisdom and philosophy into essential texts for seekers of power, understanding and mastery. Now he turns to the most important subject of all – understanding people's drives and motivations, even when they are unconscious of them themselves.

Our Rating: 4.39/5

12. The 1-Page Marketing Plan

by *Allan Dib*

To build a successful business, you need to stop doing random acts of marketing and start following a reliable plan for rapid business growth.

In The 1-Page Marketing Plan, serial entrepreneur and rebellious marketer Allan Dib reveals a marketing implementation breakthrough that makes creating a marketing plan simple and fast. It's literally a single page, divided up into nine squares. With it, you'll be able to map out your own sophisticated marketing plan and go from zero to marketing hero.

Our Rating: 4.38/5

13. Profit First

by *Mike Michalowicz*

You are about to discover the profoundly simple yet shockingly effective accounting plug-in that will transform your business from a cash eating monster into a money making a machine. In Profit First, Mike Michalowicz explains why the GAAP accounting method is contrary to human nature, trapping entrepreneurs in the panic-driven cycle of operating check-to-check and reveals why this new method is the easiest and smartest way to ensure your business becomes wildly (and permanently) profitable from your very next deposit forward.

Our Rating: 4.36/5

14. Cracking the Coding Interview

by *Gayle Laakmann McDowell*

Gayle Laakmann McDowell, the founder / CEO of CareerCup gives you the interview preparation you need to get the top software developer jobs. This is a deeply technical book and focuses on the software engineering skills to crack their interview. If you are in a business where you hire software engineers, then this is a must-read book to understand the type of software candidates that you would need to grow your business.

Our Rating: 4.34/5

15. Factfulness

by *Hans Rosling*

Factfulness is an urgent and essential book that will change the way you see the world and empower you to respond to the crises and opportunities of the future. Professor of International Health and global TED phenomenon Hans Rosling, together with his two longtime collaborators, Anna and Ola, reveal the ten instincts that distort our perspective—from our tendency to divide the world into two camps to the way we consume media (where fear rules) to how we perceive progress (believing that most things are getting worse).

Our Rating: 4.34/5

16. Football for a Buck

by *Jeff Pearlman*

In Football for a Buck, the dogged reporter and biographer Jeff Pearlman draws on more than four hundred interviews to unearth all the salty, untold stories of one of the craziest sports entities to have ever captivated America. From 1980s drug excess to airplane brawls and player-coach punch outs, to backroom business deals, to some of the most enthralling and revolutionary football ever seen, Pearlman transports readers back in time to this crazy, boozy, audacious, unforgettable era of the game. He shows how fortunes were made and lost on the backs of professional athletes.

Our Rating: 4.34/5

17. Clock Work

by *Mike Michalowicz*

Do you worry that your business will collapse without your constant presence? Are you sacrificing your family, friendships, and freedom to keep your business alive?

What if instead, your business could run itself, freeing you to do what you love when you want, while it continues to grow and turn a profit? Mike Michalowicz, offers a straightforward step-by-step path out of this dilemma. In Clockwork, he draws on more than six years of research and real-life examples to explain his simple approach to making your business ultra-efficient.

Our Rating: 4.32/5

18. High Output Management

by *Andrew S. Grove*

The essential skill of creating and maintaining new businesses—the art of the entrepreneur—can be summed up in a single word: managing. In High Output Management, Andrew S. Grove, former chairman and CEO (and employee number three) of Intel, shares his perspective on how to build and run a company.

Our Rating: 4.31/5

19. Go Pro: 7 Steps to Becoming a Network Marketing Professional

by *Eric Worre*

Over twenty years ago at a company convention, Eric Worre had an aha moment that changed his life forever. At that event he made the decision to Go Pro and become a Network Marketing expert. Since that time, he has focused on developing the skills to do just that. In doing so, Eric has touched and been touched by hundreds of thousands of people around the world. Now he shares his wisdom in a guide that will ignite your passion for this profession and help you make the decision to Go Pro and create the life of your dreams.

Our Rating: 4.30/5

20. Extreme Ownership

by *Jocko Willink*

Sent to the most violent battlefield in Iraq, Jocko Willink and Leif Babin's SEAL task unit faced a seemingly impossible mission: help U.S. forces secure Ramadi, a city deemed "all but lost." In gripping firsthand accounts of heroism, tragic loss, and hard-won victories in SEAL Team Three's Task Unit Bruiser, they learned that leadership—at every level—is the most important factor in whether a team succeeds or fails.

A compelling narrative with powerful instruction and direct application, Extreme Ownership revolutionizes business management and challenges leaders everywhere to fulfill their ultimate purpose: lead and win.

Our Rating: 4.29/5

21. The Total Money Makeover

by *Dave Ramsey*

The success stories speak for themselves in this book from money maestro Dave Ramsey. Instead of promising the normal dose of quick fixes, Ramsey offers a bold, no-nonsense approach to money matters, providing not only the how-to but also a grounded and uplifting hope for getting out of debt and achieving total financial health.

Our Rating: 4.29/5

22. High Performance Habits: How Extraordinary People Become That Way

by *Brendon Burchard*

After extensive original research and a decade as the world's highest-paid performance coach, Brendon Burchard finally reveals the most effective habits for reaching long-term success. Based on one of the largest surveys ever conducted on high performers, it turns out that just six habits move the needle the most in helping you succeed. Adopt these six habits, and you win. Neglect them, and life is a never-ending struggle.

Our Rating: 4.27/5

23. Daring Greatly

by *Brené Brown*

Researcher and thought leader Dr. Brené Brown offers a powerful new vision that encourages us to dare greatly: to embrace vulnerability and imperfection, to live wholeheartedly, and to courageously engage in our lives.

Our Rating: 4.26/5

24. Here, There & Everywhere

by *Geoff Emerick*

In Here, There and Everywhere, Geoff Emerick reveals the creative process of the band in the studio and describes how he achieved the sounds on their most famous songs. Emerick also brings to light the personal dynamics of the band, from the relentless (and increasingly mean-spirited) competition between Lennon and McCartney to the infighting and frustration that eventually brought a bitter end to the greatest rock band the world has ever known, Beatles.

Our Rating: 4.25/5

25. The Intelligent Investor

by *Benjamin Graham*

The greatest investment advisor of the twentieth century, Benjamin Graham taught and inspired people worldwide. Graham's philosophy of "value investing"

— which shields investors from substantial error and teaches them to develop long-term strategies — has made The Intelligent Investor the stock market bible ever since its original publication in 1949.

Our Rating: 4.23/5

26. Elon Musk

by *Ashlee Vance*

Elon Musk, the entrepreneur and innovator behind SpaceX, Tesla, and SolarCity, sold one of his internet companies, PayPal, for $1.5 billion. Ashlee Vance captures the full spectacle and arc of the genius's life and work, from his tumultuous upbringing in South Africa and flight to the United States to his dramatic technical innovations and entrepreneurial pursuits. Vance uses Musk's story to explore one of the pressing questions of our age: can the nation of inventors and creators who led the modern world for a century still compete in an age of fierce global competition? He argues that Musk is an amalgam of legendary inventors and industrialists including Thomas Edison, Henry Ford, Howard Hughes, and Steve Jobs. More than any other entrepreneur today, Musk has dedicated his energies and his own vast fortune to inventing a future that is as rich and far-reaching as the visionaries of the golden age of science-fiction fantasy.

Our Rating: 4.23/5

27. Sprint: How to Solve Big Problems and Test New Ideas in Just Five Days

by *Jake Knapp*

A practical guide to answering business questions, Sprint is a book for groups of any size, from small startups to Fortune 100s, from teachers to non-profits. It's for anyone with a big opportunity, problem, or idea who needs to get answers today.

From three design partners at Google Ventures, a unique five-day process for solving tough problems using design, prototyping, and testing ideas with customers.

Our Rating: 4.23/5

28. The Hard Thing About Hard Things

by *Ben Horowitz*

A lot of people talk about how great it is to start a business, but only Ben Horowitz is brutally honest about how hard it is to run one.

In The Hard Thing About Hard Things, Ben Horowitz, cofounder of Andreessen Horowitz and one of Silicon Valley's most respected and experienced entrepreneurs, draws on his own story of founding, running, selling, buying, managing, and investing in technology companies to offer essential advice and practical wisdom for navigating the toughest problems business schools don't cover.

Our Rating: 4.23/5

29. Scaling Up: How a Few Companies Make It...and Why the Rest Don't

by *Verne Harnish*

In Scaling Up, Harnish and his team share practical tools and techniques for building an industry-dominating business. These approaches have been honed from over three decades of advising tens of thousands of CEOs and executives and helping them navigate the increasing complexities (and weight) that come with scaling up a venture. This book is written so everyone — from frontline employees to senior executives — can get aligned in contributing to the growth of a firm. There's no reason to do it alone, yet many top leaders feel like they are the ones dragging the rest of the organization up the S-curve of growth. The goal of this book is to help you turn what feels like an anchor into wind at your back — creating a company where the team is engaged; the customers are doing your marketing; and everyone is making money.

Our Rating: 4.23/5

30. The Gifts of Imperfection

by *Brené Brown*

Professor Brené Brown offers a powerful and inspiring book that explores how to cultivate the courage, compassion, and connection to embrace your imperfections and to recognize that you are enough.

Each day we face a barrage of images and messages from society and the media telling us who, what, and how we should be. We are led to believe that if we could only look perfect and lead perfect lives, we'd no longer feel inadequate.

Our Rating: 4.20/5

31. Radical Candor

by *Kim Scott*

From the time we learn to speak, we're told that if you don't have anything nice to say, don't say anything at all. While this advice may work for everyday life, it is, as Kim Scott has seen, a disaster when adopted by managers.

Scott earned her stripes as a highly successful manager at Google and then decamped to Apple, where she developed a class on optimal management. She has earned growing fame in recent years with her vital new approach to effective management, the "radical candor" method.

Our Rating: 4.20/5

32. Get Over Your Damn Self

by *Romi Neustadt*

Romi Neustadt is passionate about helping others build lucrative direct sales and network marketing businesses that help create lives with more freedom and flexibility, greater purpose and a lot more fun. In this book she offers you the same direct, no-BS coaching she's given to tens of thousands to help you acquire the skills to build this sucker and teach your team to do the same. And, equally important, she'll work on your mindset so you stop overcomplicating it all and stop letting the negative voices in your head win.

Our Rating: 4.20/5

33. Principles

by *Ray Dalio*

Ray Dalio, one of the world's most successful investors and entrepreneurs, shares the unconventional principles that he's developed, refined, and used over the past forty years to create unique results in both life and business—and which any person or organization can adopt to help achieve their goals.

Our Rating: 4.19/5

34. The 48 Laws of Power

by *Robert Greene*

When it comes to morality and ethics, people are used to thinking in terms of black and white. Conversely, "The 48 Laws of Power" deals primarily with the gray areas. At the risk of sounding melodramatic and trite, we say that most of the Laws covered in this book can be used for great evil or for great good. It depends on the reader.

Each Law comes with true stories from history about those who successfully observed it and those who foolishly or naively transgressed it. Robert Greene has an interpretation for each story.

Our Rating: 4.19/5

35. Crushing It!

by *Gary Vaynerchuk*

Gary Vaynerchuk offers new lessons and inspiration drawn from the experiences of dozens of influencers and entrepreneurs who rejected the predictable corporate path in favor of pursuing their dreams by building thriving businesses and extraordinary personal brands.

In this lively, practical, and inspiring book, Gary dissects every current major social media platform so that anyone, from a plumber to a professional ice skater, will know exactly how to amplify his or her personal brand on each. He offers both theoretical and tactical advice on how to become the biggest thing on old standbys like Twitter, Facebook, YouTube, Instagram, Pinterest, and Snapchat; podcast platforms like Spotify, Soundcloud, iHeartRadio, and iTunes; and other emerging platforms such as Musical.ly. For those with more experience, Crushing It! illuminates some little-known nuances and provides innovative tips and clever tweaks proven to enhance more common tried-and-true strategies.

Crushing It! is a state-of-the-art guide to building your own path to professional and financial success, but it's not about getting rich. It's a blueprint to living life on your own terms.

Our Rating: 4.19/5

36. Traction: Get a Grip on Your Business

by *Gino Wickman*

Don't let common problems run you and your business. Get a grip and gain control with the Entrepreneurial Operating System (EOS). Inside Traction, you'll discover simple yet powerful ways to run your company with more focus, growth and enjoyment. Based on years of real-world implementation, the EOS is a practical method for achieving the business success you have always envisioned.

Our Rating: 4.18/5

37. Think and Grow Rich

by *Napoleon Hill*

Napoleon Hill was an American author who lived from 1883 to 1970. Many consider him to be the father of personal success literature.

"What the mind of man can conceive and believe, it can achieve" is one of the hallmark beliefs that provide the foundation for Hill's works. His hope was to convince the average man that success was within his reach, regardless of his circumstances.

The turning point in Hill's life was when he was assigned to interview the powerful and successful Andrew Carnegie. Carnegie believed that success could be outlined in a simple formula that anyone could understand and achieve. Napoleon Hill went on to build upon all he learned from Andrew Carnegie.

Our Rating: 4.17/5

38. Leveraged Learning: How the Disruption of Education Helps Lifelong Learners, and Experts with Something to Teach

by *Danny Iny*

Gone are the days when education was something that only happened at the start of your career. The name of today's game, both personally and professionally, is to be constantly learning: just enough, just in time, and never stopping.

Danny Iny, a successful educator entrepreneur, has been leading the charge on this growing movement. And in Leveraged Learning, he lays out the guidebook for navigating and thriving in this new world – both as a lifelong learner, and as an expert with something to teach.

Our Rating: 4.17/5

39. Secrets of the Millionaire Mind: Mastering the Inner Game of Wealth

by *T. Harv Eker*

Secrets of the Millionaire Mind reveals the missing link between wanting success and achieving it!

In Secrets of the Millionaire Mind, T. Harv Eker states: "Give me five minutes, and I can predict your financial future for the rest of your life!" Eker does this by identifying your "money and success blueprint." We all have a personal money blueprint ingrained in our subconscious minds, and it is this blueprint, more than anything, that will determine our financial lives. You can know everything about marketing, sales, negotiations, stocks, real estate, and the world of finance, but if your money blueprint is not set for a high level of success, you will never have a lot of money—and if somehow you do, you will most likely lose it! The good news is that now you can actually reset your money blueprint to create natural and automatic success.

Our Rating: 4.17/5

40. Women & Money

by *Suze Orman*

Suze Orman investigates the complicated, dysfunctional relationship women have with money in this book. With her signature mix of insight, compassion, and soul-deep recognition, she equips women with the financial knowledge and emotional awareness to overcome the blocks that have kept them from making more out of the money they make. At the center of the book is The Save Yourself Plan–a streamlined, five-month program that delivers genuine long-term financial security. But what's at stake is far bigger than money itself: It's about every woman's sense of who she is and what she deserves, and why it all begins with the decision to save yourself.

Our Rating: 4.16/5

41. Zero to One

by *Peter Thiel*

"ZERO TO ONE EVERY MOMENT IN BUSINESS happens only once. The next Bill Gates will not build an operating system. The next Larry Page or Sergey Brin won't make a search engine. And the next Mark Zuckerberg won't create a social network. If you are copying these guys, you aren't learning from them."

Peter — Thiel, Zero to One: Notes on Startups, or How to Build the Future

This book is a collection of Silicon Valley business wisdom for the startup world, based on a course that he taught at Stanford in 2012. Its contents would probably startle few people, but is very well written and richly studded with war stories from his entrepreneurial past.

Our Rating: 4.16/5

42. YouTube Secrets

by *Sean Cannell*

YouTube has changed our world—from how we view video to how we connect and market—opening a new entrepreneurial landscape to ambitious individuals. Thousands of people generate six to seven figures annually from online video content. And, with the right roadmap, you too could be en route to real influence and income.

In YouTube Secrets, online video experts Sean Cannell and Benji Travis draw on a decade of experience as well as interviews with more than one hundred top creators to give you a step-by-step YouTube success playbook.

Our Rating: 4.16/5

43. Dare to Lead

by *Brené Brown*

Brené Brown spent the past two decades researching the emotions that give meaning to our lives. Over the past seven years, she found that leaders in organizations ranging from small entrepreneurial start-ups and family-owned businesses to non-profits, civic organizations and Fortune 50 companies, are asking the same questions: How do you cultivate braver, more daring leaders? And, how do you embed the value of courage in your culture?

Dare to Lead answers these questions and gives us actionable strategies and real examples from her new research-based, courage-building programme.

Our Rating: 4.13/5

44. The Obstacle Is the Way

by *Ryan Holiday*

We are stuck, stymied, frustrated. But it needn't be this way. There is a formula for success that's been followed by the icons of history—from John D. Rockefeller to Amelia Earhart to Ulysses S. Grant to Steve Jobs—a formula that let them turn obstacles into opportunities. Faced with impossible situations, they found the astounding triumphs we all seek.

These men and women were not exceptionally brilliant, lucky, or gifted. Their success came from timeless philosophical principles laid down by a Roman emperor who struggled to articulate a method for excellence in any and all situations.

This book reveals that formula for the first time—and shows us how we can turn our own adversity into advantage

Our Rating: 4.13/5

45. Outliers: The Story of Success

by *Malcolm Gladwell*

In this stunning new book, Malcolm Gladwell takes us on an intellectual journey through the world of "outliers"–the best and the brightest, the most famous and the most successful. He asks the question: what makes high-achievers different?

His answer is that we pay too much attention to what successful people are like, and too little attention to where they are from: that is, their culture, their family, their generation, and the idiosyncratic experiences of their upbringing. Along the way, he explains the secrets of software billionaires, what it takes to be a great soccer player, why Asians are good at math, and what made the Beatles the greatest rock band.

Our Rating: 4.13/5

46. Unshakeable: Your Financial Freedom Playbook

by *Tony Robbins*

Market corrections are as constant as seasons are in nature. There have been 30 such corrections in the past 30 years, yet there's never been an action plan for how not only to survive but thrive through each change in the stock market.

Building upon the principles in Money: Master the Game, Robbins offers the reader specific steps they can implement to protect their investments while maximizing their wealth. It's a detailed guide designed for investors, articulated in the common-sense, practical manner that the millions of loyal Robbins fans and students have come to expect and rely upon.

Few have navigated the turbulence of the stock market as adeptly and successfully as Tony Robbins. His proven, consistent success over decades makes him singularly qualified to help investors (both seasoned and first-timers alike) preserve and add to their investments.

Our Rating: 4.13/5

47. Thinking, Fast and Slow

by *Daniel Kahneman*

In Thinking, Fast and Slow, Kahneman takes us on a groundbreaking tour of the mind and explains the two systems that drive the way we think. System 1 is fast, intuitive, and emotional; System 2 is slower, more deliberative, and more logical. Kahneman exposes the extraordinary capabilities—and also the faults and biases—of fast thinking, and reveals the pervasive influence of intuitive impressions on our thoughts and behavior. The impact of loss aversion and overconfidence on corporate strategies, the difficulties of predicting what will make us happy in the future, the challenges of properly framing risks at work and at home, the profound effect of cognitive biases on everything from playing the stock market to planning the next vacation—each of these can be understood only by knowing how the two systems work together to shape our judgments and decisions.

Engaging the reader in a lively conversation about how we think, Kahneman reveals where we can and cannot trust our intuitions and how we can tap into the benefits of slow thinking. He offers practical and enlightening insights into how choices are made in both our business and our personal lives—and how we can use different techniques to guard against the mental glitches that often get us into trouble. Thinking, Fast and Slow will transform the way you think about thinking.

Our Rating: 4.12/5

48. Millionaire Success Habits: The Gateway to Wealth & Prosperity

by *Dean Graziosi*

Millionaire Success Habits is a book designed with one purpose in mind; and that is to take you from where you are in life, to where you want to be in life, by using easy to implement "Success Habits" into your daily routine.

This book has broken down the walls of complexity and created simple success recipes for you to quickly implement in your life to reach the level of wealth and abundance you desire.

Our Rating: 4.12/5

49. Imagine It Forward: Courage, Creativity, and the Power of Change

by *Beth Comstock*

The world will never be slower than it is right now, says Beth Comstock, the former Vice Chair and head of marketing and innovation at GE. But confronting relentless change is hard. Companies get disrupted as challengers steal away customers; employees have to move ahead without knowing the answers. To thrive in today's world, every one of us has to make change part of our job.

In Imagine It Forward, Comstock, in a candid and deeply personal narrative, shares lessons from a thirty year career as the change-maker in chief, navigating the space between the established and the unproven. As the woman who initiated GE's digital and clean-energy transformations, and its FastWorks methodology, she challenged a global organization to not wait for perfection but to spot trends, take smart risks and test new ideas more often. She shows how each one of us can— in fact, must — become a "change maker."

Our Rating: 4.11/5

50. Man Up: How to Cut the Bullshit and Kick Ass in Business (and in Life)

by *Bedros Keuilian*

After years of coaching and consulting hundreds of startup rookies as well as seasoned entrepreneurs, executives, and CEOs, Bedros Keuilian realized that most people who want to start a business, grow an existing business, author a book, make more money, or make a bigger impact usually take the long, slow, painful way to get there . . . and more than 80 percent of entrepreneurs never get to their desired destination or achieve their full potential in business. They treat their dream as if it were merely a hobby and dip their toes in the water, but they never commit to diving in—you get the idea.

It's time to cut the bullshit excuses. Everyone has a gift, a purpose. It's your duty to figure out what your gift is and how you're going to share it with the world.

Man Up: How to Cut the Bullshit and Kick Ass in Business (and in Life) is your guide to doing exactly that. Keuilian, founder and CEO of Fit Body Boot Camp and known as the "hidden genius" behind many of the most successful brands and businesses throughout multiple industries, will show you how to break out of the sea of mediocrity, get singularly focused on your purpose, and do what it takes—not only to achieve but dominate your goals.

Our Rating: 4.10/5

51. Blitzscaling: The Lightning-Fast Path to Building Massively Valuable Companies

by *Reid Hoffman*

What entrepreneur or founder doesn't aspire to build the next Amazon, Facebook, or Airbnb? Yet those who actually manage to do so are exceedingly rare. So what separates the startups that get disrupted and disappear from the ones who grow to become global giants?

The secret is blitzscaling: a set of techniques for scaling up at a dizzying pace that blows competitors out of the water. The objective of Blitzscaling is not to go from zero to one, but from one to one billion -as quickly as possible.

Our Rating: 4.10/5

52. The Messy Middle: Finding Your Way Through the Hardest and Most Crucial Part of Any Bold Venture

by *Scott Belsky*

Entrepreneur, Chief Product Officer at Adobe, and product advisor to many of today's top start-ups Scott

Belsky believes we focus too much on the start and the finish of any project, ignoring the most important part—the messy middle—where success is truly determined.

Belsky draws on his experiences building Behance, selling it to and leading product teams at Adobe, and then working as an investor and advisor with companies like Airbnb, Pinterest, Uber, and sweetgreen to distill seven years' worth of vital insights at every stage of building a business. He features examples from some of the most interesting people and teams, from entrepreneurs to writers, from small start-ups to billion-dollar companies transforming their industries.

Our Rating: 4.08/5

53. Be Obsessed or Be Average

by *Grant Cardone*

From the millionaire entrepreneur and New York Times best-selling author of The 10X Rule comes a bold and contrarian wake-up call for anyone truly ready for success. Before Grant Cardone built five successful companies (and counting), became a multimillionaire, and wrote best-selling books, he was broke, jobless, and drug-addicted.

Obsession made all of his wildest dreams come true. And it can help you achieve massive success too. As Grant says, we're in the middle of an epidemic of average. The conventional wisdom is to seek balance and take it easy. But that has really just given us an excuse to be unexceptional.

Feed the beast: when you value money and spend it on the right things, you get more of it. Shut down the doubters – and use your haters as fuel.

Our Rating: 4.08/5

54. Rich Dad's CASHFLOW Quadrant: Rich Dad's Guide to Financial Freedom

by *Robert T. Kiyosaki*

The Cashflow Quadrant is the follow-up guide to finding the financial fast track that best works for you. It reveals the strategies necessary for moving beyond just job security to greater financial security by generating wealth from four selective financial quadrants. This work will reveal why some people work less, earn more, pay less in taxes, and feel more financially secure than others. It's simply a matter of knowing which quadrant to work in.

Our Rating: 4.08/5

55. The 7 Habits of Highly Effective People

by *Stephen R. Covey*

When Stephen Covey first released The Seven Habits of Highly Effective People, the book became an instant rage because people suddenly got up and took notice that their lives were headed off in the wrong direction; and more than that, they realized that there were so many simple things they could do in order to navigate their life correctly. This book was a wonderful education for people, education on how to live life effectively and get closer to the idea of being a 'success' in life.

Our Rating: 4.07/5

56. Start with Why

by *Simon Sinek*

Why are some people and organizations more innovative, more influential, and more profitable than others? Why do some command greater loyalty from customers and employees alike? Even among the successful, why are so few able to repeat their success over and over?

Drawing on a wide range of real-life stories, Sinek weaves together a clear vision of what it truly takes to lead and inspire. This book is for anyone who wants to inspire others or who wants to find someone to inspire them.

Our Rating: 4.07/5

57. The Power of Habit: Why We Do What We Do in Life and Business

by *Charles Duhigg*

In The Power of Habit, award-winning New York Times business reporter Charles Duhigg takes us to the thrilling edge of scientific discoveries that explain why habits exist and how they can be changed. With penetrating intelligence and an ability to distill vast amounts of information into engrossing narratives, Duhigg brings to life a whole new understanding of human nature and its potential for transformation.

At its core, The Power of Habit contains an exhilarating argument: The key to exercising regularly, losing weight, raising exceptional children, becoming more productive, building revolutionary companies and social movements, and achieving success is understanding how habits work.

Habits aren't destiny. As Charles Duhigg shows, by harnessing this new science, we can transform our businesses, our communities, and our lives.

Our Rating: 4.06/5

58. Mindset: The New Psychology of Success

by *Carol S. Dweck*

After decades of research, world-renowned Stanford University psychologist Carol S. Dweck, Ph.D., discovered a simple but groundbreaking idea: the power of mindset. In this book, she shows how success in school, work, sports, the arts, and almost every area of human endeavor can be dramatically influenced by how we think about our talents and abilities. People with a fixed mindset — those who believe that abilities are fixed — are less likely to flourish than those with a growth mindset — those who believe that abilities can be developed. Mindset reveals how great parents, teachers, managers, and athletes can put this idea to use to foster outstanding accomplishment.

Dweck offers new insights into her now famous and broadly embraced concept. She introduces a phenomenon she calls false growth mindset and guides people toward adopting a deeper, truer growth mindset. She also expands the mindset concept beyond the individual, applying it to the cultures of groups and organizations. With the right mindset, you can motivate those you lead, teach, and love — to transform their lives and your own.

Our Rating: 4.06/5

59. Grit: The Power of Passion and Perseverance

by *Angela Duckworth*

Psychologist Angela Duckworth shows parents, educators, students, and business people both seasoned and new that the secret to outstanding achievement is not talent but a focused persistence called grit.

Why do some people succeed and others fail? Sharing new insights from her landmark research on grit, Angela Duckworth explains why talent is hardly a guarantor of success. Rather, other factors can be even more crucial such as identifying our passions and following through on our commitments.

Why do some people succeed and others fail? Sharing new insights from her landmark research on grit, Angela Duckworth explains why talent is hardly a guarantor of success. Rather, other factors can be even more crucial such as identifying our passions and following through on our commitments.

Our Rating: 4.06/5

60. The 10X Rule: The Only Difference Between Success and Failure

by *Grant Cardone*

Achieve "Massive Action" results and accomplish your business dreams! While most people operate with only three degrees of action-no action, retreat, or normal action-if you're after big goals, you don't want to settle for the ordinary. To reach the next level, you must understand the coveted 4th degree of action. This 4th degree, also know as the 10 X Rule, is that level of action that guarantees companies and individuals realize their goals and dreams.

The 10 X Rule unveils the principle of "Massive Action," allowing you to blast through business clichZs and risk-aversion while taking concrete steps to reach your dreams. It also demonstrates why people get stuck in the first three actions and how to move into making the 10X Rule a discipline. Find out exactly where to start, what to do, and how to follow up each action you take with more action to achieve Massive Action results.

Our Rating: 4.06/5

61. Good to Great: Why Some Companies Make the Leap and Others Don't

by *Jim Collins*

To find the keys to greatness, Collins's 21-person research team read and coded 6,000 articles, generated more than 2,000 pages of interview transcripts and created 384 megabytes of computer data in a five-year project. The findings will surprise many readers and, quite frankly, upset others.

Our Rating: 4.06/5

62. The Lean Startup: How Today's Entrepreneurs Use Continuous Innovation to Create Radically Successful Businesses

by *Eric Ries*

Most startups fail. But many of those failures are preventable. The Lean Startup is a new approach being adopted across the globe, changing the way companies are built and new products are launched.

Eric Ries defines a startup as an organization dedicated to creating something new under conditions of extreme uncertainty. This is just as true for one person in a garage or a group of seasoned professionals in a Fortune 500 boardroom. What they have in common is a mission to penetrate that fog of uncertainty to discover a successful path to a sustainable business.

Our Rating: 4.06/5

63. Awaken the Giant Within

by *Anthony Robbins*

Anthony Robbins shows you his most effective strategies and techniques for mastering your emotions, your body, your relationships, your finances, and your life. He provides a step-by-step program teaching the fundamental lessons of self-mastery that will enable you to discover your true purpose, take control of your life, and harness the forces that shape your destiny.

Our Rating: 4.06/5

64. The Fifth Risk

by *Michael Lewis*

What are the consequences if the people given control over our government have no idea how it works? Michael Lewis's brilliant narrative takes us into the engine rooms of a government under attack by its own leaders.

Willful ignorance plays a role in these looming disasters. If your ambition is to maximize short-term gains without regard to the long-term cost, you are better off not knowing those costs. If you want to preserve your personal immunity to the hard problems, it's better never to really understand those problems. There is an upside to ignorance and downside to knowledge. Knowledge makes life messier. It makes it a bit more difficult for a person who wishes to shrink the world to a worldview.

Michael Lewis finds them, and he asks them what keeps them up at night.

Our Rating: 4.05/5

65. How to Make Sh*t Happen

by *Sean Whalen*

Is your daily life chaotic and out of control?

Do you struggle with work/life balance?

Does it feel like there are never enough hours in the day to accomplish all your goals?

Does it feel like no matter how hard you try it's never good enough?

Are you looking for a simple yet executable roadmap to create the life you've always desired?

If you answered "yes" to any of these questions, then you need… HOW TO MAKE SH*T HAPPEN.

Our Rating: 4.04/5

66. Kitchen Confidential: Adventures in the Culinary Underbelly

by *Anthony Bourdain*

A deliciously funny, delectably shocking banquet of wild-but-true tales of life in the culinary trade from Chef Anthony Bourdain, laying out his more than a quarter-century of drugs, sex, and haute cuisine—now with all-new, never-before-published material.

New York Chef Tony Bourdain gives away secrets of the trade in his wickedly funny, inspiring memoir/expose. Kitchen Confidential reveals what Bourdain calls "twenty-five years of sex, drugs, bad behavior and haute cuisine."

Our Rating: 4.04/5

www.ingramcontent.com/pod-product-compliance
Lightning Source LLC
Chambersburg PA
CBHW021833110526
R18278200001B/R182782PG44588CBX00009B/13